MEDIUMSHIP
RAISING THE STANDARDS

Exercise Book 2

Mediumship Raising The Standards

Copyright © Tim Abbott 2017 All Rights Reserved

The rights of Tim Abbott to be identified as the author of this work have been asserted in accordance with the Copyright, Designs and Patents Act 1988

All rights reserved. No part may be reproduced, adapted, stored in a retrieval system or transmitted by any means, electronic, mechanical, photocopying, or otherwise without the prior written permission of the author or publisher.

Spiderwize
Remus House
Coltsfoot Drive
Woodston
Peterborough
PE2 9BF

www.spiderwize.com

A CIP catalogue record for this book is available from the British Library.

The views expressed in this work are solely those of the author and do not necessarily reflect the views of the publisher, and the publisher hereby disclaims any responsibility for them.

ISBN: 978-1-911596-52-3

MEDIUMSHIP
RAISING THE STANDARDS

Exercise Book 2

TIM ABBOTT

Can I take this opportunity to thank those who have
supported me during the writing of this book.

Appreciation to my family, thanks to my wife Janette for her
invaluable input and a special thanks to my daughter Beckie
for her endless hours of work and transcribing of this book.

Extended thanks to my past and present
students who continue to inspire me.

Contents

Chapter 1

INTRODUCTION

Throughout this book, we will be exploring and looking at many different aspects of mental mediumship. This book has been designed with education in mind. Whilst I respect there are two main expressions of mediumship, both physical mediumship and mental mediumship, within this book we will be focusing upon mental mediumship.

So, let us look at what mental mediumship is – it is believed and accepted that the spirits of our ancestors can communicate with those who are sensitive enough to have an awareness of that higher frequency (mediums).

This phenomenon, which has been practiced for centuries, is referred to as mental mediumship simply because the medium perceives, as part of the process, both the information and indeed individuals from the spirit world through the faculties of their own mind. The definition of mediumship is to mediate from one state of life to another. In other words a medium, through their sensitivity, psychic faculties and awareness (awareness being where you perceive the information through the faculties of your mind) will perceive either information or an individual from the spirit world and relay that information to a recipient (i.e. achieving the expression of mediumship).

The mediums' desire and goal at any given time throughout their development and demonstration of mediumship should always be to prove beyond reasonable doubt that we understand as the incarnate spirit, if you like, the life force of god that abides within every living being survives that which we understand as physical death and retains that divine life force and their own individual intelligence and personality. Whilst we accept the physical brain ceases to function at the point of physical death, the soul, which is understood as the thinking, intelligence and personality aspects of the incarnate spirit, survives physical death and is a crucial facet of what now becomes the discarnate spirit, which is why as mediums we accept that the spirit world is a world of intelligence.

Through the process of mediumship these individuals who step forward to communicate from the spirit side of life and through their intelligence have the ability to relay factual information (i.e. personal information about themselves such as memories gathered within their lifetime, maybe memories shared with the recipient, detailed information about their death or indeed about their life, knowledge of current affairs in the client's life and much more) to prove both the presence and the very existence of the said spirit communicator. This can be limited depending on how developed the individual medium is. This information is known by mediums as evidence, which equals proof of survival.

We use a vast range of communication methods on the earth plane daily: radio, TV, telephones, computers, email, text messaging, the internet and many more. Why would this be any different for the spirit world? They will use many different forms of communication depending on the individual spirit's ability and knowledge, the ability of the medium and the particular subject of the information and the best method of serving it.

So, let us look at some of the different types of mental mediumship that mediums use to articulate mediumship. There is that which is known as clairvoyant mediumship (known to some as evidential mediumship), trance, healing, inspirational writing, the expression of spiritual philosophy (which is a beautiful form of mediumship), one-to-one sittings and platform demonstrations. Evidence can be found within all of these different expressions of mediumship.

A word to the wise

Although I have been aware of the spirit world since I was a child and my earliest memories of interacting with the spirit world were from the age of seven, I have been formally studying mediumship since the age of 19, since 1979. So for approximately 37 years I have been involved in the demonstrating of mediumship in one form or another, and I have been teaching mediumship for 25 years. I am proud to say that my work has taken me to many different countries throughout the world and to some of the most established and recognised schools and colleges of mediumship, and I would like to share some of the dos and don'ts of mediumship that I have learnt along the way.

If, like me, you are somebody who has decided to dedicate yourself to your mediumship, I ask that during your development, your demonstrations, or any time you are articulating your mediumship that you give yourself over to that experience 100% and with every aspect of your being, putting any other facets of your life, be they financial, family, or work-related, to one side whilst you do so. However, whilst mediumship is an important part of your life, I ask you to focus on the word PART. Mediumship is simply a part of your life and it cannot and should not become the whole of your life, as there are other aspects of your life that, just like your mediumship, need focusing on, for example family life, work and finances. This is something that you will need to review from time to time just to make sure that you are, to the best of your ability, keeping all that is in your life in balance.

Your mediumship will become enriched through your life experiences and if you are not allowing yourself to live your life because you are too busy doing your mediumship, your mediumship is in danger of becoming shallow and lifeless. There is a saying between students that some mediums have got their head in the spirit world so much that they forget to live, so please don't allow this phrase to relate to yourselves.

Throughout this book, you will find evidential exercises to enrich your mediumship, but please never forget that factual evidence is only but one aspect of evidence when bringing the presence of spirit. Also, allowing your recipient to feel the love and the presence of their loved one is equally as important as the facts and figures, so please allow both the evidential and the spiritual evidence equally to be a part of your mediumship.

As a student of mediumship you will find and meet teachers who will inspire you and whilst I encourage students to find a teacher like this and study with them, please be careful not to mimic or take on board traits or habits that your teacher may already possess. I think it is important that you allow your personality, your energy and your own spirit to be a part of your mediumship, and don't fall into the trap of adopting somebody else's personality, energy and traits as part of your spiritual development. Please remember the spirit world loves and respects your teacher for who they are and, equally, the spirit world loves and respects you for who you are. The spirit world wishes to work with you and not a carbon copy of your teacher.

Mediumistical development and spiritual unfoldment should run parallel as you move forward on your mediumistical journey. It is important for any student of mediumship to adopt patience. Please do not be in a hurry to reach the destination within your mediumistical journey.

There is no pinnacle to mediumship and you will find that, no matter how many years you study and practice mediumship, there will always be an opportunity to further learn and develop if you are of a mind to do so, as the opportunity for spiritual or mediumistical growth, just like life, is eternal.

During a meditation I once asked my guide Edward, "Please

give me some advice that I can relay to my students to help them in their development." Edward shared the following information with me:

"Please tell your students to stop looking for the phenomena during the act of mediumship, stop looking for the telephone number or the full name as part of the factual evidence, stop looking for the full materialisation as part of the physical mediumship, stop looking to heal the broken bones within the act of healing, simply look for the company of spirit, and when you have the company of spirit in its purest sense then all the phenomena that you desire will naturally follow. Without the company of spirit you cannot practice mediumship. Far too often students put the evidence and the result before the spirit. Put the spirit before the evidence and the result, and all will be well."

Each time you blend and connect with the spirit world in whatever format, be it for meditation, inspiration, or the act of mediumship in its many forms, it is a unique, magical and individual experience, so please remember what you are achieving through your mediumship. You are proving beyond reasonable doubt to the world that the continuation of life beyond physical death is a reality and that in itself is a small miracle. Let us never lose sight of that.

Through your mediumship, you have the potential to change people's lives, possibly to save people's lives. Through each expression of mediumship that you give allow the love, the life force and the presence of spirit to be an essential part of the very essence of each demonstration.

Throughout my career as a medium I have run many courses and written a previous book entitled *Mediumship – Raising the Standards – Exercise Book 1*, and throughout my teaching career I have endeavoured to do that very thing for students, raise their standards. I do hope that this book and its exercises can inspire you to enrich the quality within your mediumship thus raising the standards of your own ability. I ask you not to simply read this book at face value and use the exercises as they are presented in this book, but to alter the exercises to suit your own personality and style of mediumship and to use them to inspire yourself with your own challenges.

CHAPTER 2

GLOSSARY OF TERMS

Throughout this book, you will find that I will use terminology that is familiar to mediumistical and spiritual groups and circles, and the following definitions will help and guide you through the book and give you a greater understanding of the science within mental mediumship.

Attunement

Attunement is a method of adjusting the mental processes from the active conscious to the passive conscious, which brings about an awareness through the sensitivity of the unseen individuals and information that either abides within or is expressed from the spirit world.

Awareness

Awareness is an activity of the medium's mind or consciousness, acknowledging, yet not interfering with, the effect and the changes to the sensitivity of the medium due to the blending of spiritual energy, which can come about with the awareness of either incarnate or discarnate spiritual energies.

Blending

Blending is where the energy's space and sensitivity of both the medium and the discarnate communicating spirit share the same spiritual space (this does not mean the discarnate spirit steps inside the physical body of the medium) to bring about interaction.

Communicator

The communicator is the individual (or individuals) from the spirit world who is expressing their presence and information (i.e. communicating with the medium).

Development

Development is the studying and practice of the individual's mediumistical ability with the aim to strengthen and further both their psychic and mediumistical ability. There are three recognised levels of development: beginners, intermediate and advanced. A beginner is an individual who whilst he or she may have some natural mediumistical abilities, they don't know how to either use or put them into practice and would need guidance from a tutor. An intermediate is an individual who has studied mediumship for some time, possibly several years, and has the ability to attune themselves to the spirit world, have the company of somebody from the spirit world and express their experience (articulate mediumship), whereas an advanced individual is someone who has studied mediumship for several years and has the ability to attune themselves to the spirit world, have the company of somebody from the spirit world and maximise the relationship between themselves and the communicator, thus maximising the quality and depth of information and evidence they express through their mediumship.

Energy

Spirit energy is life force made manifest. From a material perspective energy is perceived through example, as light or heat, yet is not of matter. From a spiritual point of view the spirit world and all that it is, is spiritual energy and can only be perceived through sensitivity.

Evidence

Evidence is the information that is expressed by the medium to the recipient on behalf of the communicating spirit and is an expression of the intelligence of that individual communicating spirit.

Guide

A guide is a discarnate spirit that is spiritually developed and highly evolved and will form a partnership with the developing medium to support, guide and inspire the medium both in their mediumistical development and in their spiritual unfoldment.

Incarnate/Discarnate Spirit

Incarnate spirit refers to the life force, expression of god or spirit that abides within and as an aspect of the physical existence. Discarnate spirit gives reference to the spirit that has taken its transition from the physical body at the point of physical death and abides within that which we understand is the spirit world.

Meditation

Meditation is both a practice and a discipline to further and advance the unfoldment of one's awareness of both themself and of the spirit world. During the practice of meditation, the spiritual senses that are used within mediumship will naturally become heightened and strengthened. Meditation will raise your awareness beyond the daily and conscious vibrations and take you to those spiritual vibrations that are more familiar within the practice of mediumship.

Mediumship

The definition of mediumship is to mediate from one state of life to another through one's sensitivity and awareness.

Message

The message is an aspect of the demonstration by a medium and can be defined as the reason for coming. When we move beyond the evidence and information that a medium expresses to prove they have a discarnate spirit with them, what is it the individual spirit has come to say?

Psychic faculties

A psychic is a person who has the ability to use **extrasensory perception** to identify information hidden from the normal senses. The individual will perceive the psychic experience through the spiritual senses. This can and will come about on both the psychic and mediumistical levels of perception. The spiritual senses are as follows:

CLAIRVOYANCE = Vision of spiritual energy

CLAIRSENTIENCE = Sensing of spiritual energy

CLAIRAUDIENCE = Hearing of spiritual energy

CLAIRGUSTANCE = Tasting of spiritual energy

CLAIRALIENCE = Smelling of spiritual energy

Recipient

The recipient is the individual who receives the demonstration (message) which is delivered from the medium.

Remote viewing

Remote viewing can be experienced both psychically and mediumistically – psychically where by the medium or psychic takes their awareness to a distant location and, using their spiritual senses, journeys through a point within that location (e.g. a building, a park or a town). Mediumistically remote viewing is where, through the interaction between a medium and an individual from the spirit world (discarnate spirit), the individual takes the medium on a journey through a location of importance that is relevant to that which they are expressing to the recipient (e.g. a building, a park or a town).

Sensitivity

Every living being is sensitive in various degrees. Within mediumship our sensitivity is used like a tool through our inner senses to sense non-physical vibratory emanations.

Spirit world

The spirit world is that state of existence that is not of the physical matter or conscious. Its very existence and location is not of some heavenly point beyond the horizon but indeed shares the same space of existence that we inhabit but exists upon a different frequency and different vibrations, which is why it is not perceived by the physical senses.

Syntax

Syntax is a journey through evidence (i.e. the way the spirit world express through their intelligence the information and evidence and the unfolding story of the message).

CHAPTER 3

WHY DO YOU WISH TO BE A MEDIUM?

When I was 19, after several years of being pestered by the spirit world to do mediumship and after agreeing with the spirit world that I would dedicate myself to the development and demonstrating of mediumship, one of my guides mentioned to me, "Don't ever allow your mediumship to become a parlour trick." For years I didn't quite understand the full depth of that statement but now I believe I am beginning to get a grasp of what it was he was trying to relay to me.

I think it is important that from time to time during our journey of development we stop and contemplate on why we feel the need or wish to be mediums. I believe everyone who embarks upon the experience of developing their mediumistical abilities does so for very personal and individual reasons. For some, it's simply a wish to serve the spirit world, whereas for others it may be that they are looking to understand the experiences and mediumistical gift that they have. Some individuals may need to feel the love and embracement that can only be felt whilst in the company of the spirit, and for others maybe the lure of the fame that mediumship can sometimes bring is a temptation.

Throughout the years of my teaching of mediumship, I have come to understand that for most students of mediumship it is indeed a combination of several, if not all the above, in various degrees and levels depending on the individual. For all mediums I believe there is a desire to be in that altered state (mediumistical state). Whilst within that spiritual energy and having the company of the individual from the spirit world – this in itself can be quite addictive and, certainly in my own individual case, after doing a demonstration I'm not analysing how good or bad I felt I did, but thinking where and when my next demonstration is, and I believe what I'm actually thinking to myself is when I will get my next high from the company of spirit. I think it's important that we keep a perspective on our relationship with the spirit world and the activity of our mediumship, whilst mediumship is an important part of our lives it is only a part of our lives.

Each time we demonstrate our mediumistical abilities and each time through our mediumship an individual from the spirit world is accepted by a recipient, we are not simply stating, "Oh look at me, I'm a good medium because I am just proving to you who I have from the spirit side of life." The reality is much greater than that. Each time we demonstrate our mediumship and prove beyond reasonable doubt who we have from the spirit side of life, we are, through spiritual science (the act of mediumship), proving that that spirit that abides within each living being is eternal.

A medium's goal should first and always be to prove the existence of the discarnate spirit, the reality of the spirit world and to bring spiritual upliftment to the recipient. We must look at the subject of financial payment. I love the quote in the book So you want to be a Medium by W.H. Evans: "If you worship the alter you should be kept by the alter". What W.H. Evans is saying in his book is there are many spiritual people who are paid for their services and indeed some will have a weekly wage. We need to look no further than vicars and priests who charge for their services. If you wish to organise a wedding, a funeral, a baptism or naming service, there is a set fee for the vicar, minister or priest who will take the service, so why can a medium not charge for their services? I'm a great believer that mediums should not charge for their mediumistical ability but have the right to charge for their time. If you go to a garage to have your car fixed there will be an hourly rate. If you hire a gardener to tidy the garden there will be an hourly rate. If you jump in a taxi you will pay for the time and the mileage, not for their skills and labour, so why not a medium?

In my opinion, mediums should always be careful that they don't allow the financial gain to become the factor that drives their mediumship. Of course, like any trade, mediums have a right to be paid for their labour, but the art of mediumship is not simply a practical skill. Mediumship is, indeed, a practical ability but it is also a spiritual gift that carries a spiritual philosophy, so we must not allow ourselves to be blinded by the financial reward but look equally at the spiritual rewards both for ourselves, the client, and indeed the spirit world.

Mediums have a natural ability through their sensitivity to take their awareness to a frequency or level that is unattainable to most people, and with this awareness and sensitivity coupled with their development of mediumship and the company of individuals from the spirit world, they can articulate their craft of mediumship, hopefully always giving value to the spirit world and not lowering their standards to parlour tricks.

Exercise 1a

An exercise for all levels which can be done in either a large group or in pairs.

Discuss why you feel you want to be a medium and/or the importance of mediumship. You can vary the length of time taken up by each student depending on their level of ability.

Exercise 1b

An exercise for intermediate or advanced students.

Give students the same subject matters – "why you feel you want to be a medium?" and/or "the importance of mediumship" – and ask them to take these titles away with them and to format an address or some philosophy on the above subjects. For the intermediate student, this can be a 10-minute address. For the advanced student this can be a 15-minute address to be presented the next time they are in circle, group or class.

This exercise will give them both the confidence of speaking in a public arena and allowing themselves to be inspired by spirit.

CHAPTER 4

THE NATURAL PROCESS OF MENTAL MEDIUMSHIP

Whilst I understand many of you who have studied *Exercise Book 1* would have already read this chapter, I believe it is important that we remind ourselves of the natural process of mental mediumship, and for those of you who are joining me for the first time, it is important that you understand this natural process to give value to the following subjects and exercises within this book.

It is important that we understand the process through which the practice of mediumship comes about.

Through the development of an individual's sensitivity (i.e. psychic ability) and the inclusion of the presence of spirit, the individual has the potential to put into practice the art of mediumship.

The spirit communicator will express their presence, personality and thoughts as the energy to the medium, who then perceives the energy through their Clairvoyant, Clairaudient and Clairsentient abilities (i.e. psychic abilities).

Sensitivity

and

Awareness

can bring about

The Possibilities of Psychic Experiences

and, in harmony with your

Spiritual Attunement...

this can bring about

The Potential for the Act of Mediumship.

*Only when the medium expresses his or her
experiences of spirit comes about the*

Practice of Mediumship

Sensitivity

Have you noticed how a mushroom, through its sensitivity, will react to the morning dew? It becomes more open within its structure. And have you been aware of how a flower, through its sensitivity, reacts to the rain?

Each and every one of us is sensitive. How we use that sensitivity differs from person to person. Through exercises and regular development, students who are studying their psychic and mediumistical abilities come to accept and indeed work with their sensitivity. Let us look at the human aura:

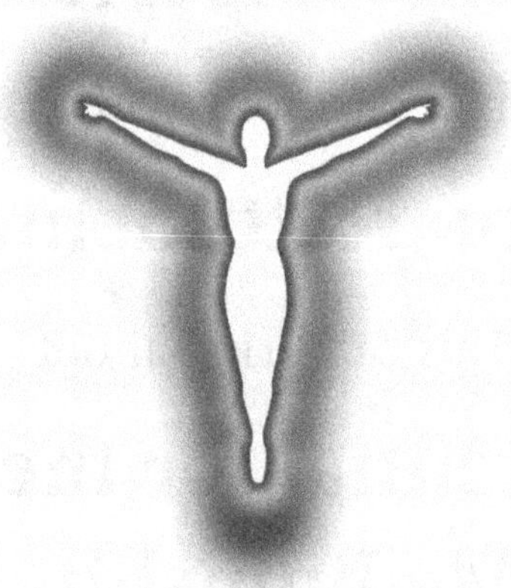

From the early 1940s for many years, the Russian husband and wife team Semyon and Valentina Kirlian (Kirlian photography) did in depth research on the auric field, discovering that plants, animals and indeed human beings have an auric field.

This is an electromagnetic energy field which is sensitive to other energies that either blend or impinge upon it. In my understanding, the auric field is made up of many different ingredients of energy, which include Mental Energy (the energy created through our thought process), Physical energy (the energy created through our physical body), Emotional energy (created within our emotions) and Spiritual energy (the energy emanating from our own incarnate spirit). All of these will abide within the auric field.

These different energies will fluctuate and change from time to time per the natural changes and experiences that come within an individual's life, for example, if an individual suffered a bereavement through the loss of a loved one this would affect their emotional energy, therefore changing the level of emotional energy within the auric field.

With this understanding of the auric field we must remember that the spirit world is both a world of intelligence and a world of energy, therefore when some individual steps forward from the spirit world to communicate through mediumship there is what is termed "a blending of energies" (i.e. auric fields between both the medium and the communicator). This blending will bring about a change or an effect upon the auric field and the **Sensitivity** of the medium.

Awareness

Awareness is an activity of the medium's mind or consciousness, acknowledging, yet not interfering with the affect and changes to the sensitivity of the medium due to the blending of spiritual energy (possibly an individual from the spirit world). Through extensive development, the student of mediumship learns not to change the effect to his or her sensitivity with their own thoughts, logic or conclusion yet simply be aware of the changes within their own sensitivity. This can come about through **the possibilities of psychic experiences**.

Although there are several, the five main senses that can come about through the psychic abilities of either the psychic or medium are those known as:

CLAIRVOYANCE = to clearly see the spiritual energy.
CLAIRSENTIENCE = to clearly sense the spiritual energy.
CLAIRAUDIENCE = to clearly hear the spiritual energy.
CLAIRGUSTANCE = to clearly taste the spiritual energy.
CLAIRALIENCE = to clearly smell the spiritual energy.

It is believed that these phrases were introduced by the Marquis de Fuysegur in the eighteenth century. If we take for example a medium when interacting with an individual from the spirit world, the effect the individual has upon the medium's sensitivity is first experienced through the auric field. This can then be perceived through the psychic senses. For example, the medium may see the presence of the spirit communicator, sense the presence of the communicator or hear the presence of the communicator.

Spiritual Attunement

It is understood that the spirit world shares the same space as we do within our own physical existence, however the frequency of the energy in which the spirit world exists moves at a different pace to the frequency of energy that we exist within.

It is understood that the frequency of energy within the spirit world is both finer and faster than that of ours, and therefore individuals who have not developed their mediumistical abilities would not normally be aware of that finer vibration (the spirit world). Through different exercises and therefore development of their sensitivity, a medium develops the ability to attune to the spirit world (Spiritual Attunement).

Trained mediums have developed the ability to take their

awareness to that finer vibration that exists as part of the spirit world.

The Potential for the Act of Mediumship

The definition of mediumship is to mediate from one state of life to another. During the act of mediumship, a medium relays to a recipient what he or she is aware of through their sensitivity and psychic senses whilst in the company of an individual from the spirit world, and through the intelligence or thought process of that individual, what it is they wish to relay to the said client. It is only when the medium is expressing the thoughts of the communicator that this is defined as the act of mediumship.

If we keep in mind the process of mediumship, there are various opinions on the question as to whether mediums are born or developed. Whilst I accept mediums are probably born with a potential, that potential needs to be developed into an ability.

If we take, for example, the famous violinist Nigel Kennedy, whilst he showed great musical potential as a young boy, he still attended and studied at the Yehudi Menuhin School of music then later at the Juilliard School in New York, fine tuning his musical ability, turning it from a potential into a wonderful ability.

Mediumship is no different. I would always recommend students of mediumship find a development circle under the guidance of a good tutor. Each time we are in the company of spirit, be it for the sake of an exercise or simply for the beauty of the company of spirit, we are both exercising and strengthening and therefore developing our Sensitivity, Awareness, Psychic Abilities and the art of mediumship.

Whilst I am sure the spirit world has some input and influence as to what type of medium we become, equally I believe our personality, energy and mindset will naturally have an influence as to what type of mediumship we are naturally drawn to. However, how far we develop our mediumship is our responsibility. It is important that we feed and nurture our potential. We feed our potential through mediumistical exercises and we nurture our potential by simply being in the company of spirit.

So now hopefully we can see the value of different exercises and how they can improve and strengthen both our relationship with the spirit world and our mediumship. The exercises within this book are suitable for mental mediumship (clairvoyant mediumship).

Through partaking in these exercises, our goal is to heighten our sensitivity. Added to this, the strengthening of our awareness, the understanding of our own psychic abilities and the ability to be, and stay, within the company of spirit, as well as developing a professional approach to the presentation and delivery of mediumship.

CHAPTER 5

EVIDENCE AND ITS MANY DIVERSE ASPECTS

I have always taught and promoted that evidence is an expression of the intelligence of the individual communicating spirit and within that expression there are many different facets of evidence.

If we accept the intelligence within the presence of spirit, then we must accept that the individual communicator from the spirit world will express their story's information and evidence in a rich and diverse manner. Below are some examples of how the spirit world may communicate.

1. Factual

(e.g. I have your father here from the spirit world and he tells me his name is Thomas.)

2. Emotional

(e.g. Your mother from the spirit world is expressing happiness and she tells me that you're recently married.)

3. Spiritual

(e.g. Your mother tells me that you lived at number 75 Parkside Road but this house was more than just a house as it was a home full of family love.)

4. Symbolic

(e.g. I can see a horse in a very small field with high fences and I can feel, like the horse, that you are feeling trapped at the moment.)

5. Subjective

Any information that is simply the communicator's opinion (e.g. I was a loving husband).

So, let me offer you some exercises to cover some of these different expressions of evidence:

Exercise 2a

An exercise for subjective evidence, suitable for beginners, this exercise is suitable for either the platform or as a one-to-one sitting exercise.

Ask the student to verbally express their philosophy on a set subject. This exercise is for 5 minutes and it is important that they fill the 5 minutes with their verbal input. At the end of the 5 minutes, bring the exercise to a close and discuss the exercise afterwards. Did the student manage to fill the 5 minutes? Did they take time initially to build their own spiritual power and did they stay within the power through the duration of the exercise? If the students are in pairs they can change roles and repeat.

Exercise 2b

Suitable for intermediate students, this exercise is best suited to a one-to-one sitting environment. The duration of the exercise should be approximately 15 minutes.

Once the student who is working first has established the communicator from the spirit world (i.e. the client knows who the communicator is) and after approximately 10 minutes of working, the working medium should invite the client to direct the medium back to a piece of evidence that they have already offered up as part of the exercise, using the piece of evidence as a subject matter. For example: If the working student offered up a piece of evidence such as "your grandfather is talking about memories on the farm and apple picking in the orchard", the client may pick the subject matter of "orchard", with this is mind allowing the communicator, not the working student, but the communicator, to give their philosophy on the said subject, in this case, "orchard".

At the end of the 15 minutes the student can bring the sitting to a close. If they wish to they can introduce at the end of the sitting a message (reason for coming) from the communicating spirit. Discuss your findings. For example, during the philosophy from the communicator did the client observe both the personality and the intelligence of the communicating spirit that they know and remember so well and did the message tie in with or relate to the philosophy? Change roles and repeat exercise.

Exercise 2c

An exercise suitable for advanced students. This exercise is best suited in a one-to-one sitting environment, and the duration of the exercise should be approximately 20 minutes.

Once the student who is working first has established the communicator from the spirit world (i.e. the client knows who the communicator is) and after approximately 10 minutes of working, the working medium should invite the client to direct the medium back to a piece of evidence that they have already offered up as part of the exercise, using the piece of evidence as a subject matter. For example, if the working student offered up a piece of evidence such as "your grandfather is talking about memories on the farm and apple picking in the orchard", the client may pick the subject matter of "orchard".

At this point, the working student, through the power of their mind, invites the communicator to step back; not to go back to the spirit world but simply to put some distance between themselves and the working student. Following this, the working student will spend approximately 3 minutes giving their philosophy on the chosen subject and after the agreed time has lapsed, the working student will invite the individual from the spirit world to step closer once again to strengthen the blending between communicator and working student. Then the working student can invite the individual from the spirit world to give their philosophy on the same chosen subject, again for approximately 3 minutes.

After the duration of 3 minutes this must naturally move into the reason for coming (i.e. message). Bring your exercise to a close and discuss your findings. For example, could the recipient feel the presence of their loved one? Were the philosophy from the working student and the individual communicating from the spirit world different? If so, how? Once you have completed discussing your findings, you can change roles and repeat the exercise.

If we look at exercises for factual evidence, adjusting the length of time of the exercise from between 10-20 minutes depending on the level of the student's ability, the following exercise is suitable for either platform or one-to-one sittings.

Exercise 3

For the beginner, after establishing who the communicator is, give two factual full statements (i.e. evidence relating to the communicator). Neither statement must be connected to each other and then and only then can the working student naturally go to the reason for coming and bring the exercise to a close. It is important during these exercises that each statement is a full and in depth statement. The same exercise can be used for intermediate students but instead of two statements, encourage them to give three, and with advanced students, encourage five.

It is important that you encourage these statements to be

unique and individual and naturally offered up by the individual communicating from the spirit world. This will encourage the student to be factual in their delivery as and when necessary.

I have highlighted five different facets of evidence and it is important that you explore and practice each type within your studies and development of your mediumship so that you can allow these different types of evidence to be a natural part of your mediumship, bringing depth and clarity and the presence, intelligence and personality of each individual spirit as a crucial part of your delivery.

Moving on to look at how we present this evidence, I believe as mediums it is important that we embrace the fact that when we are demonstrating our mediumship we are the voice and the representation for an individual from the spirit side of life who has no voice, no personality and no intelligence other than that which we allow to be expressed though our mediumship.

It is therefore vital that we give ourselves over to the experience of delivering that of which the individual wishes to be expressed 100%, so how we deliver the evidence is very important to give value to that which is being expressed and indeed not to devalue through lack of ability. I remind you, the world of spirit is a world of intelligence and just like us, individuals in the spirit world are not one dimensional and will express themselves in many diverse ways and within that expression will be the individual's logic, reasoning, emotional input, educational input and personality. So, I think the following is something worth studying and looking at.

PRESENTING THE EVIDENCE

Whilst there are different types of evidence such as factual, spiritual and emotional evidence, and many more, there are only a few ways to verbally present it. Depending on how we present it, it can give value or indeed de-value the evidence.

1. **The One-worded Statement** – You can understand "August" as an anniversary (August being the one word). This has very little value as evidence if any at all.

2. **The Full Statement** – You would understand that your father is in the spirit world and he died of cancer at the age of 67. This statement expresses the intelligence of spirit (in this case the intelligence of father). This expression of mediumship has good value.

3. **The Story** – This is where the medium verbalises a full in-depth story on the spirit communicator's chosen subject. The story could be of any and indeed many aspects of the communicator's life (work, family, finances, illnesses, memories etc.). When the evidence is expressed in this manner it has great value.

When we look at any form of evidence it gains in value (for the recipient) when presented both through natural syntax, through the intelligence of spirit, and in the right order.

The following exercises are suitable in pairs (i.e. one-to-one sittings):

Exercise 4

For beginners, I wish each student to tell a 3-minute funny story, event or memory that has happened in their life. It is important that they fill the 3 minutes, during which I invite them to give in-depth factual information thus bringing the story alive.

For intermediates, I would like the student to give two 3-minute stories, one being funny, and one being something that they are proud of. It is important that they fill each 3 minutes, giving two full individual stories from their life.

For the advanced, give three 3-minute stories, one being funny, one being serious, and the third and final story being something they are proud of from their life. It is important that they fill each 3 minutes giving depth and being factual within each story.

These exercises have been stories from the lives of the individual students. For the intermediate and advanced students, we can further these exercises by doing it in the company of somebody from the spirit world. Once the student has proven who they have from the spirit world they can invite the communicator to give one or two in depth stories from their own life, remembering that the communicator can express in depth stories from their lives in the same manor that you, the student, expressed your own prior to this part of the exercise, which would then be followed by the reason for coming, then bringing the exercise to a close.

I ask you to remember that evidence is expressed in many ways through many forms of mediumship. Do not simply limit yourself to the exercises I have offered up in this chapter but to look at different forms of mediumship and the evidence that is expressed within those facets of mediumship.

CHAPTER 6

THE USE OF REMOTE VIEWING WITHIN MEDIUMSHIP

Remote viewing is the practice of seeking impressions about a distant or unseen location, object or individual using subjective means, in particular, **psychic abilities.**

It is generally understood that psychics are still today employed by certain government agencies within different countries to remote view upon information within different countries for security reasons. However, remote viewing can equally be used as a facet of mediumship whereby the communicator will express a location of importance that is relevant to their life or to the reason why they are communicating, for example their home, place of work or place where they socialised, and the medium, through the power of their awareness and sensitivity will journey through that location whilst verbally expressing what it is they are experiencing.

It is important that we don't limit our remote viewing abilities simply to locations. Whilst remote viewing can be very beneficial to a location, equally, you could remote view an object. For example, if a lady stepped forward from the spirit world and she was holding a handbag, why not remote view the objects within the handbag. The contents of any lady's handbag or gentleman's wallet would tell you a lot about them. Yes, there would be the usual items like make up and perfume but there probably will also be items such as a driving licence. A driving licence has a name upon it, maybe shopping receipts which would highlight what shops the communicator shopped in, maybe a bus or train ticket which would highlight what bus or train they travelled on or possibly a personal diary or notebook which you could remote view for information.

Why not remote view objects within the location? For example, if you were in the kitchen, you could open the cupboards to see what type of food has been bought, or what kind of medication is stored in the medicine cabinet. I'm sure you will have had the experience in your life of walking into a room and feeling the atmosphere and knowing there has just been an argument or heated conversation in that room. I believe the phrase is "you could cut the atmosphere with a knife" so why not do that within your mediumship? When you are remote viewing a location, feel the atmosphere and feel the energy within that location. Was it a happy home? A happy workplace? Remember, energy is not restricted to time so you could remote view the energy within that location whilst at the same time taking your awareness back in time. Has this location always been a happy place? If not, why? Are you aware of shifts within the energy in that location? If so, why?

I'm sure you would have heard of psychometry, where by a psychic or medium will hold an object of a recipient, possibly a piece of jewellery or a photograph, and through their sensitivity become aware of the energy that is an aspect of the object, gathering information of the history and owner of the said object. With this in mind, why not psychometrize an object within a location that you are remote viewing during the act of mediumship, thus bringing more depth to the remote viewing.

There are times when a communicator would show you a location where they died. For example, through your awareness you may find yourself in a car with the communicator and you find yourself describing the journey you are both taking which sadly ends in a collision and the passing of the said communicator. Don't restrict your remote viewing to the journey. Have a look at the surrounding views – are you in the countryside or the city? Through your senses have a look at the sky, the trees and the plants. What time of day is it? What time of year is it?

Let me offer you some exercises ranging from beginners through intermediate to advance and enrich your mediumistical ability of remote viewing.

Exercise 5a

For beginners, this exercise is suitable in pairs and will be a 10-15-minute exercise for each student.

Put yourselves in pairs and decide who will work first and who will work second. The student who works first we will call student number 1 and the student who works second, we will call student number 2.

Student number 1 will close their eyes, relax their mind and attune themselves to the energy of student number 2, knowing in their mind that somewhere during this practice they will become aware of the information of a location of importance for student number 2. The moment student number 1 perceives any information of a location they need to begin to verbalise what they are experiencing, and through the power of their sensitivity, journey through that location always verbalising their journey.

After approximately 5 minutes, as long as student number 2 can accept the location, student number 1 knows within their mind that they are taking their awareness away from student number 2 and taking it to the spirit world, at the same time asking that an individual in the spirit world who is connected to the location that they have just expressed and or connected to the recipient step forward from the spirit world and make their presence known. As soon as student number 1 becomes aware of the individual from the spirit world, they express what and who they are experiencing. After approximately a further 5 minutes they bring the exercise to a close, discuss their experiences with their recipient and then change roles and repeat the exercise.

Exercise 5b

For intermediates, the following exercise is suitable for either platform demonstration or one-to-one sittings. This is a 20-minute exercise for each student.

As always, put yourselves in pairs and decide who is going first, and again as always, we will refer to the student going first as student number 1.

Student number 1 will make a link with the spirit world for somebody that student number 2 can relate to; a family member, a friend or a colleague. After approximately 10 minutes of student number 1 expressing evidence to prove the communicator to the point where student number 2 is comfortable that they know who the communicator is, from that point on student number 1 will invite the communicator to take them "mediumistically" to a place of importance.

During the act of remote viewing the location, I would like student number 1 to become aware of different objects within the location, remote viewing the objects and expressing their experience of the object to student number 2, and once student number 2 has accepted at least 2 different objects, student number 1 can then naturally move on to the reason for coming (the message) and bring this exercise to a close. Discuss your experience and change roles and repeat the exercise.

Exercise 5c

For advanced students, the following exercise is suitable for both platform demonstration and one-to-one sittings. This is a 20-minute exercise for each student.

Again, if we look at it from a one-to-one sitting point of view, student number 1 will make a connection with an individual in the spirit world who is in one way or another connected to student number 2. Once student number 2 is comfortable they know who the communicator is, student number 1 can invite the communicator to take them to a place of importance.

Whilst remote viewing the location, student number 1 must ensure that the communicator journeys through the location with them at all times. After approximately 5 minutes and once student number 2 is comfortable that they know of the location, student number 1 must turn their attention to the communicator and ask the communicator to give an in-depth story about the location, for example, maybe the history of the location, who lived there, who worked there, maybe a factual memory. Once student number 1 has exhausted the story they can naturally move to the reason for coming (the message) and bring this exercise to a close. Discuss your experience, change roles and repeat the exercise.

Remote viewing can be a beautiful aspect of mediumship as it has the potential to bring depth and factual information as part of your demonstration or sitting. Please allow these three exercises to inspire you with your own exercises.

CHAPTER 7

SPIRITUAL HEALING

There are many forms of healing such as reiki healing, crystal healing, sound healing, trance healing and many more. Because we are focusing upon mental mediumship within this book we will look solely at spiritual healing.

Spiritual healing, like all forms of mental mediumship is where the medium attunes themselves to the spirit world and allows a blending from an individual from the spirit world and themselves to come about whilst being disciplined to hold a passive state for the expression of mediumship through the act of healing.

It is quite often the case that the individual who steps forward from the spirit world to deliver the healing is somebody who would often work in partnership with the medium and has, over a period of time, built a rapport and trust within their working relationship, thus allowing the energy and practice of healing to move freely without interference from the medium and through the medium's ability. This can quite often be a guide who has some medical knowledge.

It is sometimes seen that healing is the poor relative of mediumship and, in some cases, is perceived as not being mediumship at all. In my opinion this could not be further from the truth. Healing is in my opinion the purest form of mediumship that exists and my logic behind that statement is as follows. As we know, there are two forms of mediumship – mental and physical mediumship – and on the whole, mediumship either falls into one category or the other depending on the nature of its expression. However, healing can and does from time to time sit in both categories at the same time.

The practice of spiritual healing is mental mediumship but the result of spiritual healing can quite often be physical mediumship. We have all heard the stories of individuals who have cancerous growths and the doctors have said there is nothing we can do for you yet after the individual receives healing the doctors discover the cancerous growth has shrunk – an example of physical mediumship. This is the only form of mediumship that covers both mental and physical at the same time.

Here are some exercises with healing in mind.

Exercise 6a

This exercise is suitable for beginners and suitable in pairs.

Decide between yourselves who is going to work first and who is going to work second. The student who is working first must take time to attune themselves to the spirit world keeping in mind that an individual will step forward to give healing to the recipient. However, whilst attuning yourself to the spirit world, I would ask you to send a request out that one of the loved ones of your client who is in the spirit world step forward to give the healing (not one of your guides).

After the blending has come about, allow the healing to proceed for approximately 10-15 minutes, after which bring the healing to a close, the exercise to an end and discuss your findings. For example, did your client recognise the individual from the spirit world who was giving them healing? After this you can change roles and repeat the exercise.

Exercise 6b

This exercise is suitable for intermediates in pairs.

Decide between yourselves who is going to work first and who is going to work second. The student who is working first must take time to attune themselves to the spirit world keeping in mind that an individual will step forward to give healing to the recipient. However, whilst attuning yourself to the spirit world, I would ask you to send a request out that one of the loved ones of your client who is in the spirit world step forward to give the healing (not one of your guides).

After the blending has come about, allow the healing to proceed for approximately 15 minutes. After the 15 minutes have lapsed, take your attention to and begin to interact with the communicator and for the following 5 minutes verbalise from the communicator the reason for coming (the message). After this, bring the healing to a close, the exercise to an end and discuss your findings, for example – did your client recognise the individual from the spirit world who was giving them healing? Could the reason for coming be accepted? After this you can change roles and repeat the exercise.

Exercise 6c

This exercise is suitable for advanced students in pairs.

Decide between yourselves who is going to work first and who is going to work second. The student who is working first must take time to attune themselves to the spirit world keeping in mind that an individual will step forward to give healing to the recipient, however whilst attuning yourself to the spirit world, I would ask if you will send a request out that one of the loved ones of your client who is in the spirit world step forward to give the healing (not one of your guides).

After the blending has come about, allow the healing to proceed for approximately 15 minutes, which must be done in the silence. After the 15 minutes has lapsed, allow the communicator to step even closer to you and allow yourself to be inspired with what it is the communicator wishes to talk about to their loved one, your client, for approximately 5 minutes. Please remember that the words that are expressed from the loved one will be of a healing nature and spiritual in style. Now take your attention to and begin to interact with the communicator and for the following 5 minutes verbalise from the communicator the reason for coming (the message). After which bring the healing to a close, the exercise to an end and discuss your findings. For example, did your client recognise the individual from the spirit world who was giving them healing? Was the inspirational talking from the medium relevant and valuable to the client and could the reason for coming be accepted? After this you can change roles and repeat the exercise.

CHAPTER 8

TRANCE

There are four states of consciousness within the human brain: Beta, Alpha, Theta and Delta. Most mental mediums, whilst in the practice of mediumship, will find themselves in the state of consciousness known as Theta, however, those mediums who practice Trance will normally find themselves in the state of consciousness known as Delta which is also the same state of consciousness that we are in when we are asleep or indeed unconscious.

Through the development of trance, the medium learns to attune themself to the delta state of consciousness whilst naturally allowing the blending of an individual from the spirit world. Through this deep passive state that the medium finds themself in, the communicator is allowed to bring about a very close blending between themself and the medium, which in turn allows the communicator to express their personality, their intelligence and their thoughts through the ability of the medium without the thoughts, input or interference of the medium. Because of this when mediums are practicing trance there is less of an awareness by the medium of the process of the mediumship or indeed what is being verbalised by the communicator during the act of trance.

There are many different expressions of the phenomena of trance, that is to say how the communicator from the spirit world will express themselves whilst the medium is in trance, for example, healing, automatic writing, clairvoyant trance and philosophy. Each time a medium sits for trance they should never dictate which form of trance mediumship should take place but instead leave themselves open to the direction of the spirit world.

The following exercises are of a clairvoyant trance nature. That is to say when the medium has moved into the trance state and an individual steps forward from the spirit world (possibly a guide), that individual will give an evidential clairvoyant message attaining to somebody else in the spirit world that the recipient would be able to clearly understand from the evidence and facts that the communicator has offered up whilst the medium sustains the trance state.

These exercises are of an experimental clairvoyant trance nature and suitable for both intermediate and advanced trance students and suitable in pairs.

Exercise 7a

Decide between yourselves who is going first and who is going second. The student who is working first must naturally allow themselves to move into the trance state and allow the close blending between themselves and the communicator to come about and accept that at some time following the blending the communicator will communicate verbally with the client (the communication will be of a general nature).

After approximately 3 minutes of verbal communication, the recipient is to ask the communicator, "Can you go back to the spirit world and gather some information about one of my loved ones in the spirit world?" (do not dictate which loved one), after which the communicator will re-establish a blending with the medium who has sustained the trance state during this process, having no input at all, equally assuming nothing for the duration of the exercise. For a further 10 minutes the communicator will verbalise information and evidence about one of the client's loved ones from the spirit world, after which the client will thank the communicator and invite them to step away from the medium and return to the spirit world allowing the medium to gently come out of the trance state bringing the exercise to an end. Discuss your findings, change roles and repeat the exercise.

Exercise 7b

Decide between yourselves who is going first and who is going second. The student who is working first must naturally allow themselves to move into the trance state and allow the close blending between themselves and the communicator to come about and accept that at some time following the blending the communicator will communicate verbally with the client (the communication will be of a general nature). After approximately 3 minutes of verbal communication, the recipient is to ask the communicator, "Can you go back to the spirit world and gather some information about one of my loved ones in the spirit world and bring both the information and my loved one back from the spirit world with you?" (do not dictate which loved one), after which the communicator will re-establish a blending with the medium who has sustained the trance state during this process having no input at all, equally assuming nothing for the duration of the exercise, and for a further 5 minutes the communicator will verbalise information and evidence about one of the clients loved ones from the spirit world.

After approximately 5 minutes the client is to simply ask the communicator to step back from the medium and allow the loved one to step forward and blend with the medium, after which the loved one can express whatever they wish to verbalise. Following this, the client will thank the communicator and invite them to step away from the medium and return to the spirit world, allowing the medium to gently come out of the trance state bringing the exercise to an end. Discuss your findings, change roles and repeat the exercise.

CHAPTER 9

PRACTICAL EXERCISES FOR BEGINNERS, INTERMEDIATE AND ADVANCED

I have dedicated this chapter solely to practical exercises. The following exercises cover many aspects of mediumship and will help to bring depth of quality and clarity to your mediumship and help the unfolding process of development.

I encourage you to study all the exercises within this chapter. Whilst I appreciate you may be an intermediate or advanced student of mediumship you may find some of the exercises that are listed for beginners may very much suit your personal needs. Can I recommend that you read and understand fully each exercise before putting them into practice?

The first group of exercises are looking at how we can format and make a sitting or demonstration easier through its delivery. Please study the following structure to guide you through the following exercises.

Messages Made Easy

Messages and information given from the world of spirit, like a story, letter or newspaper article will unfold naturally with a beginning, middle and end. Here is one example that may help you with structure and direction when giving a message.

1. **COMMUNICATOR** *(Male or female)*

2. **PERSONAL INFORMATION RELATING TO THE COMMUNICATOR** *(Physical description, age, how they passed, relationship to the recipient)*

3. **WHAT THE COMMUNICATOR WISHES TO TALK ABOUT** *(Memories, anniversaries, support or concern for a loved one)*

4. **HOW THE COMMUNICATOR (not the medium) WISHES TO BRING THE COMMUNICATION TO A CLOSE** *(Goodbye)*

As a student/medium when working with a natural structure to your messages you will make it easier for the world of spirit, you the medium and your recipient to understand the information relayed by the communicator.

Exercise 8a

An awareness exercise suitable for beginners.

This exercise is best presented in a group setting. Place the chairs in two circles – an inner circle and an outer circle with the chairs facing each other so the inner circle is facing the outer circle and vice-versa – positioned for one-to-one sittings but to form a circle. Whilst being in one large circle, you are working in pairs. Those students on the inner circle will be the mediums first. The student is to go into the quiet and to become aware of their own spiritual energy. It is important that you give time for the student to do this.

When the student begins to have an experience of their own energy they are to verbalise to their partner what it is they are experiencing and after maybe a minute of them describing their experience, direct the student to go back into the quiet and simply to dwell in their own energy for approximately 1 minute, then through the power of their mind to invite an individual from the spirit world to step forward to blend with the student's energy. Whilst you do not want the student to interact with the communicator at this point, invite the student once again to become aware of their own energy. Has it changed because of the company of the individual from the spirit world? If so, how?

Invite the student to verbalise the changes within their own energy to their client. Allow them to do this for approximately 1 minute, then invite the student to take their awareness back to their own energy and back to their visitor from the spirit world. Encourage the student to interact with the communicator for approximately 1 minute, then invite them to verbalise what they are aware of with their visitor from the spirit world to the client for approximately 1 minute. It matters not if the client recognises the communicator or not as this is not an exercise of mediumship but is an awareness exercise.

Once the student has finished and invited the visitor to go back to the spirit world, invite all the students who have just worked to stand and move clockwise on chair and repeat exercise. This will be done three times, after the third time encourage the students to talk about their experiences. Bring the exercise to a close, change seats with your partner and those students now on the inner chair can repeat the exercise.

Exercise 8b

An exercise suitable for intermediate students.

This exercise is suitable in pairs, and each exercise should have a 20-minute duration. Before starting the exercise discuss and look at the natural format of a sitting.

Decide between the students who will work first and who will work second, using this format throughout the sitting. Each time the student working finishes a particular section within the format, they must go back to the spirit communicator and ask a question on something the individual presented to them within that particular section and then present the answer to the client.

This must be done with all four sections and after approximately 20 minutes bring the sitting to a close, discuss your findings, change roles and then repeat the exercise.

This exercise will encourage the student to interact with the communicator naturally as and when it is necessary.

Exercise 8c

An exercise suitable for advanced students

The following exercise involves philosophy within your mediumship. Depending on how many students are in the group or circle, this exercise is suitable for either platform or a one-to-one sitting environment. Decide who is going first and ensure the student has time to attune themselves to the spirit world and proceed with the sitting or demonstration. After the student who is working has secured a recipient and the recipient is comfortable they know who the communicator is, the student is to continue with approximately five individual statements of factual information relating to the communicator which the recipient can accept. At this point the student invites the recipient to highlight one of the five statements that they wish the medium to focus upon as a subject matter for philosophy and at this point the student invites the communicator to step back (not to return back to the spirit world, just step back) and for an agreed period of time, I would recommend 3-4 minutes, the student is to give their philosophy on the chosen subject matter.

When the chosen period of time has lapsed, the student invites the communicator to step forward once again (give time to bring this about) then the student invites the communicator to express their philosophy on the same subject matter which the student expresses, ideally filling the chosen period of time. When the chosen period of time has lapsed, the student can naturally move into the reason for coming (the message), bring the exercise to an end, and discuss your findings. Two of the questions you should be discussing are "Was the recipient aware of the difference within the philosophy between the medium and the communicator?" and "When the communicator was expressing their philosophy was the personality and intelligence of the communicator expressed through the philosophy?" Finally, bring your discussion to a close and change roles.

Exercise 9

An exercise suitable for all levels of students

The following exercise includes both clairvoyant mediumship and meditation as part of the same exercise.

Put the students into pairs and between them decide who is going to work first and proceed in giving each other, one after another, a 15-minute sitting. **Please do not discuss any of the findings at this point.** After each student has received a sitting from their fellow student, both students are to sit for meditation for approximately 10 minutes and during the meditation the student is to send their thoughts to the spirit world, inviting whoever the communicator was in the clairvoyant sitting they received from their fellow student prior to the meditation to step forward and join them in their meditation.

As soon as the student becomes aware of their loved one from the spirit world, they simply invite their loved one to continue the subject matter, evidence and discussion you were offering up during the sitting prior. After approximately 10 minutes, you bring yourselves back, or if there is a tutor overseeing this exercise the tutor can invite students to bring their meditation to an end and when, and only when, you are fully conscious you can discuss your findings with your fellow student.

Exercise 10

An exercise suitable for beginners

This exercise requires at least two people and will need to be done in pairs. One will fulfil the role of a director and the other will be the student. It will also require one blindfold and four plain A4 sheets of paper – each sheet of paper to be of a different colour. The student is to put on the blindfold, removing the sense of sight thus encouraging and heightening the sensitivity within the student.

The director places one random sheet of paper in the hands of the student, ensuring that at no time the student sees the colour of the paper, and inviting the student to simply become aware of the energy that is emanating from the colour on the paper, leaving them to do so for approximately 1 minute. The director then encourages the student to verbalise (without suggesting what colour they think it is) what they are experiencing. Are they visualising anything? Are they feeling a frequency or temperature emanating from the paper?

Whatever the student is experiencing they are to be encouraged to verbally express it. Finally they are to be encouraged to express which colour they believe the paper to be. This process can be repeated with different random coloured paper as many times as necessary to suit the individual student's needs. After this process is complete the student can remove the blindfold (be aware it may be bright to the eyes after removing blindfold). Discuss your findings with each other and change roles.

Exercise 11

An exercise suitable for intermediate students

This exercise is suitable for either platform work or in a one-to-one sitting session, preferably a one-to-one sitting lasting for 25 minutes. For this exercise we will call the two students student one and student two. Student one, without linking to the spirit world at all, is to spend 5 minutes telling student two a funny story or event from their own life. It is important that they give full details and descriptions so as to make the story very clear, and to fill the 5 minutes allocated to this aspect of the sitting. This should immediately be followed by student one attuning themself with the spirit world and inviting somebody from the spirit world who is connected to student number two to step into their awareness.

During the following 20-minute sitting, student number one must be aware within the information and evidence offered up by the communicator when and where there is the opportunity to tell a full in depth story (presented in the same depth of information as to their own story which they presented prior to the sitting). After approximately 15 minutes, and hopefully at least one story from the communicator's life, student one can naturally move to the message (reason for coming) and bring the sitting to a natural end. Discuss your findings and change roles.

Exercise 12

An exercise suitable for upper advanced students

This exercise is suitable for either platform work or in a one-to-one sitting session. This is a 20-minute exercise and needs the discipline of the student to allow the communicators to express their stories without the influence of the student at any given time. The student, after attuning themselves with the spirit world, is to invite an individual from the spirit world who is closely connected to the recipient. When and only when, through the information and evidence offered up to the recipient, the recipient understands who the communicator is, the student invites the communicator to step back, however not to return to the spirit world, simply to step back.

The student then continues the exercise by inviting a second communicator from the spirit world to step forward: an individual who is closely connected to the first communicator. When and only when the recipient understands who the second communicator is, the student invites the second communicator to step back, not to return back to the spirit world, but to simply step back.

As soon as this process is complete the student can invite the first communicator once again to step forward into the student's awareness. The student is to then invite the communicator to express a story or event that was life changing for them. After expressing the story or event to the recipient, the student invites the first communicator to step back and the second communicator once again to step forward into the student's awareness.

The student then invites the second communicator to express how the story or event in the first communicator's life affected their life and equally express that to the recipient. This should be followed naturally by the message (reason for coming). Bring the exercise to a close, discuss your findings and change roles.

Exercise 13

An exercise suitable for all levels of students

This exercise will partly be done as a group, and partly as a one-to-one sitting. Firstly, the group needs to sit in a large circle and each student will need pen and paper. As a group, I would like each student to go into the quiet and attune themselves to the spirit world with the idea in mind that one of their loved ones (don't dictate which one) will step forward from the spirit world. Please don't try to interact or gather information from the communicator. As the loved one steps forward from the spirit world, simply allow a close blending to come about between yourself and the loved one.

Pick up the pen and paper and begin to write, knowing that, through the blending you have with your loved one, the spirit communicator will inspire you with the words that you write. Here is a wonderful opportunity for your loved one to write you a letter from the spirit world. After approximately 15 minutes know that the letter will come to an end. At no time during this exercise should you mention to any of your fellow students who the loved one is or the contents of the letter as this can be discussed at the end of the exercise.

When the letter has naturally finished, find yourself a fellow student from the group and put yourselves into pairs where you will proceed to give each other a one-to-one sitting. Decide between yourselves which student will work first and whoever is working first take time attuning to the spirit world. As you do so, send out a request to the spirit world that your communicator be the loved one who blended with your recipient earlier and wrote them their letter. At this point, decline from trying to get any evidence from the communicator but just simply allow the blending to come about between yourself and the communicator and simply begin to speak to your recipient, knowing that the communicator is inspiring you with the words you are speaking, so through your mediumship, your communicator is expressing what they wish to talk about to their loved one – your recipient. Here is a wonderful opportunity for your client's loved one simply to talk to them.

I would suggest you spend about 5 minutes allowing yourself to be inspired by your client's loved one, which you can express through the spoken word after. You can then bring the sitting to an end and discuss your findings with your client. For example, did your client feel that the individual who wrote them a letter and the individual who spoke through your mediumship were one and the same person? Were the nature of the letter and the nature of the spoken word one and the same subject? After you have discussed this with your recipient you can change roles and repeat the exercise.

Exercise 14

An exercise suitable for beginners

This exercise has been designed to encourage the spiritual senses within our mediumship. To be carried out within a group environment. The students must ensure that they take time to attune to the spirit world, thus activating their mediumistical ability, their sensitivity and their awareness. The student is to invite one of their guides to step forward from the spirit world into their awareness and, using the five spiritual senses (seeing, hearing, smelling, tasting, and sensing), they are to build a relationship with the guide.

After approximately 5 minutes they can end this exercise, inviting the guide to return to the spirit world, immediately after which they are to place themselves into pairs and, one after another, describe to their partner what it was that they saw, heard, smelled, tasted and sensed. They can further advance this exercise by one of the students within the pair repeating the exercise, but instead of asking for a guide, asking for somebody from the spirit world that is connected to their partner.

On becoming aware of the individual from the spirit world, the student is to use their senses as naturally as possible to build a relationship with the communicator for approximately 2 minutes, and after the time has elapsed, the student can invite the communicator to step away and return back to the spirit world, immediately afterwards describing what they experienced and who they experienced from the spirit world to their partner. The partner is to acknowledge if they understand who the communicator was. Bring the exercise to an end and discuss your findings, change roles and repeat the exercise. _

Exercise 15

An exercise is suitable for either beginners or intermediate students

This exercise is suitable for pairs. However, one chair must be placed behind the other so they are both facing the same direction, tandem like. The student in front we will call student number one and the student behind, student number two.

The student behind must be silent at all times and proceed by either sending healing to the student in front (student number one) or becoming aware of somebody from the spirit world and sending through the power of their mind (without verbalising at all) a clairvoyant sitting.

After approximately 5 minutes, bring the exercise to an end and student number one is to describe what kind of energy they felt through their sensitivity during the exercise and as to what type of sitting they felt they received, either a healing or a clairvoyant sitting. This is to be repeated three times with student number two choosing randomly which type of sitting they wish to offer up at any given time.

After the three sittings have been completed, discuss your findings and change roles.

Exercise 16

An exercise is suitable for intermediate students

This exercise is suitable for groups. Before starting the exercise, as a group discuss the subject of anniversaries and share within the group some of the important anniversaries within your life (please don't simply share that March 3rd is an important anniversary for yourself). Share with the group the anniversary, why it's important, if it involves any other people, etc. For example, a wedding anniversary would involve your spouse.

After this discussion, put yourselves into pairs and decide who is going to work first and who will work second. The student who is working first must give time to attune themselves to the spirit world, inviting somebody from the spirit world who is connected to their recipient to step into their awareness and proceed with the sitting.

During the sitting, accept that the spirit world can express and talk about different anniversaries within their own life. When these anniversaries are expressed, please ensure that you give a full statement relating to the anniversary being expressed by the communicator. Hopefully, you can do this twice within the sitting you are doing. After approximately 15 minutes, move naturally to the message (reason for coming) and bring the sitting to a close, discuss your findings, change roles and repeat the exercise.

Exercise 17

An exercise is suitable for upper advanced students

This exercise is suitable for either platform work or in a one-to-one sitting session. This exercise is to encourage depth and story within your remote viewing ability. This is a 20-minute exercise and after the student has attuned themselves with the spirit world and invited an individual from the spirit world into their awareness, they are to proceed with the demonstration or sitting.

Once, through the information offered up, the student has secured a recipient and the recipient is comfortable they know who the communicator is, the student is to invite the communicator to take them to a place of importance. Please remember, a place of importance could be a family home, workplace, place of social activity or a place that holds important memories. Please leave it for the communicator to decide what constitutes a place of importance to them. Once the client understands the place of importance, the student is to become aware of objects of importance within the location and to invite the communicator to tell the history or story behind the said object.

I would recommend that you locate at least two objects within the place of importance and, as long as the recipient is comfortable with the object and information, you can naturally move to the reason for coming (message) and bring the demonstration or sitting to a natural end. Discuss your findings with your partner and change roles.

Exercise 18

An exercise suitable for beginner students

Before starting this exercise please study the structure of a sitting – "Messages made easy" at the beginning of this chapter.

As a student/medium, when working with a natural structure

to your messages, you will find it is easier for both the world of spirit, you the medium and your recipient to understand the information relayed by the communicator.

This exercise is suitable in pairs and each exercise should have a 15-minute duration. Take time to attune to the spirit world and once you are comfortable you have a communicator from the spirit world, follow the format provided in "messages made easy" and after approximately 15 minutes bring your sitting to an end, discuss your findings and change roles.

Exercise 19

An exercise suitable for intermediate students

This exercise is best presented in a group setting. Place the chairs in two circles: an inner circle and an outer circle with the chairs facing each other so the inner circle is facing the outer circle and vice-versa, positioned for one-to-one sittings but to form a circle.

Whilst being in one large circle, you are working in pairs. Those students on the inner circle will be the mediums first. Whoever is overseeing the exercise needs to have several pieces of paper. On each piece of paper is written an individual sense. For example, on one piece "clairvoyance", another may be "clairsentience", on another "clairaudience", but all five senses must be written individually on different pieces of paper and placed face down on a surface so that the working student cannot see which sense it written on the paper.

The student who is working will give three 10-minute sittings and after each 10-minute sitting has elapsed, they will bring the sitting to a close and move clockwise one chair and repeat the exercise. However, before each 10-minute exercise, the working student must pick up one of the pieces of paper and highlight to their recipient which sense is written on the paper, and whichever sense is listed on the paper is the sense they must solely use during that 10-minute sitting. After the three

10-minute sittings have elapsed, as a group they can discuss their findings and change roles.

Exercise 20

An exercise suitable for advanced students

This exercise is suitable for either platform work or in a one-to-one sitting session. The following exercise will be a 20-minute exercise. The student who is working is to take time to attune themselves to the spirit world, invite an individual from the spirit world to blend with them and then to proceed with the sitting or demonstration.

After the student who is working has secured a recipient and the recipient is comfortable that they know who the communicator is and after approximately 10 minutes have elapsed, the student can then invite the recipient to pose a question to the communicator (I suggest this be a question that is not serious or life changing in its nature); a question that is personal to the recipient. For example, if the recipient had recently moved home they may pose the question "what do you think of the family house?" or if the recipient had recently gone through a separation or if a family member had moved away from the family unit the recipient may pose the question "how do you feel about the family at the moment?"

After the question has been verbalised by the recipient, it is important that the medium keeps in mind that the spirit world is a world of intelligence and has the ability to answer the question indirectly by sharing an experience or story from their own life that is both relevant and goes someway to answering the question that was posed by the recipient.

After the story has been expressed by the medium, the medium can naturally move forward to the message (reason for coming), bring the exercise to a natural close. Discuss your findings with your partner or recipient and change roles.

Exercise 21

An exercise suitable for advanced students

This exercise is suitable for a one-to-one sitting and will take approximately 25 minutes. Before you start the exercise, each student will need the following handout:

Monitoring your own senses

The spiritual senses are experienced within and through the psychic faculties (your sensitivity) which every human being has. Therefore, within our mediumistical work we can possess and experience all of the spiritual senses.

Are you working with your spiritual senses to their full potential?

As mediums, it is important from time to time to remind ourselves of all the senses within our sensitivity and to reconfirm that we have the potential to use all of them naturally at any given time within our mediumship.

To assist you with the following exercise, you will need to copy the table provided and use it as a tick-box exercise which may be helpful when giving each other feedback. The table is used to record which spiritual senses the medium is naturally using during the exercise and therefore, which senses they need to work upon to strengthen their mediumship.

SPIRITUAL SENSE	MEANING	YES/NO?
CLAIRVOYANCE	SEEING	
CLAIRAUDIENCE	HEARING	
CLAIRSENTIENCE	SENSING	
CLAIRGUSTANCE	TASTING	
CLAIRALIENCE	SMELLING	

Put yourselves into pairs and decide who is going to work first (with the student who is working first taking time to attune to the spirit world) and, through the power of your mind, invite somebody from the spirit world who is connected to your recipient to step forward from the spirit world to blend with you, and proceed to give an evidential sitting to your client.

After approximately 5 minutes, hopefully your client will understand who the communicator is through the evidence that you have offered them so far, after which take your awareness back to your communicator to gather a further piece of evidence. However, before verbalising this piece of evidence to your recipient, once again take your awareness back to that piece of evidence but, in your mind, know that you will be using one of the senses listed on your handout to investigate, explore and expand the evidence that you previously perceived.

Whichever sense you have used, tick where necessary on your handout as long as your recipient can accept the now enriched piece of evidence you offer up to them and continue with the sitting as naturally as possible (giving no thought to the senses) for approximately one minute. After one minute take your awareness back to your communicator to gather a further piece of evidence just like before and, before verbalising this piece of evidence to your recipient, take your awareness back to the evidence, knowing in your mind that you will use one of the remaining four senses on your list to investigate, enrich and explore the evidence.

Once you have done this you can verbalise the enriched piece of evidence to your client and tick off the necessary sense from your list. Repeat this exercise until you have exhausted all the senses on your list then you can naturally move to the reason for coming (the message), spending approximately 5 minutes on the message. Bring the sitting to an end, discuss your findings, swap places and repeat the exercise.

Exercise 22

An exercise suitable for beginner students

This exercise is suitable for a one-to-one sitting environment. One of the challenges that students who are beginning their journey of development have is the ability to blend with an individual from the spirit world consistently. Sometimes, for a beginner, a technique is required and the imagination can be used as a tool to provide an individual technique for each individual student.

Before the exercise starts, the tutor's goal is to ask each individual student to share with the group something they really enjoy doing away from mediumship and for the tutor to use what the student expresses as a technique for the individual student to bring about the company of somebody from the spirit world. For example, if a student expressed that they loved walking in the countryside, the tutor may suggest that as a technique for attunement. The student could imagine they are walking In the countryside at their favourite time of day and year and at their favourite location, and when through the power of their imagination, they can feel the beauty of the walk then simply in their mind invite somebody from the spirit world who is connected to the recipient to join them on their walk in the countryside, or if it's a student who enjoys fishing, the spirit world can join them on the bank of the river. Maybe an individual simply enjoys reading a book at home – they could invite somebody from the spirit world to sit and enjoy the book with them.

What the student is doing, through the power of their imagination, is inviting an individual from the spirit world into their happy place. The moment they become aware of the communicator they simply verbalise what and who they are aware of to the recipient, and I would suggest the student repeat this exercise three times, each time with a different recipient, remembering the aim of this exercise is not to give a full sitting but to strengthen the student's attunement and blending with an individual from the spirit world.

After the exercise is finished, discuss your findings and if necessary change roles. As the student develops they will find they need to rely on the technique less and less, and the ability to attune and blend with the spirit world will become more natural.

Exercise 23

An exercise suitable for both beginner and intermediate students

The following exercise is suitable for both beginners and intermediates, and is presented in two different formats: one for you to do at home on your own and the second to be done as part of a group. For this exercise to have value, I would recommend that the first part be done at least once a fortnight for approximately six months.

The first exercise – I would like you to write a demonstration (a message) of mediumship as if you are delivering it from a platform. This can be done from the comfort of your own home. It is important that you write the whole delivery (message) from start to finish, including the evidence followed by the message in its entirety. On the completion of this, place pen and paper down and take a 10-minute break (have a tea or coffee) and, after your break, go back to your work and read through what you had previously written, but this time read it as if you are a recipient receiving the message.

As a recipient, if there are any points within the delivery of your message where you feel you need more depth of information, underline with pen that particular section of writing. On completion of the demonstration of the message, where you have underlined is where in reality you will need to take your attention back to the communicator to get greater depth of information.

As I have already suggested, if you repeat this exercise over an extended period of time, you will find that those areas of writing that should be underlined will become less and less, and the depth of information within the writing will become greater.

The second exercise is for a group session. Depending on how many students are in the group I would suggest that you limit the people writing the role play message to five, so after the students have written and completed the examples of a demonstration (message) you will have five examples of mediumship. Each of the 5 students will stand and deliver their demonstration individually and during each delivery the group will discuss where they would want more depth of information, at which point the student underlines with pen that particular section of writing.

Continue with all five students and, on completion, discuss your findings, remembering the aim of these two exercises is to enrich the quality of delivery and the value and depth of information within the information and evidence that you deliver. Always remember that these two exercises, whilst they have value are only role playing.

Exercise 24

An exercise suitable for intermediate to advanced students

This exercise is designed to enrich the spiritual senses we use within our mediumship. Depending on how many students are in the group or circle, this exercise is suitable for either platform or a one-to-one sitting environment. Decide who is going first and ensure the student has time to attune themselves to the spirit world and proceed with the sitting or demonstration.

When the student has secured a recipient and the recipient is comfortable they know who the communicator is, the tutor or circle leader at this point advises the student as to which spiritual sense they are to solely work with within the demonstration or sitting from this point on. For example, if the tutor advises clairvoyance, the student focuses on solely seeing the information that is being expressed by the spirit communicator.

Depending on the level of ability the student who is working has within their mediumship, the tutor may choose several different senses throughout the exercise, which is to be followed with the reason for coming (the message). Discuss your findings and change roles or invite a new student to demonstrate.

Whilst we have encouraged the senses mechanically it is important to remember that when working with your clairvoyant mediumship (evidential mediumship), the senses will be activated naturally without the medium having to give any thought to the process.

The following handout is to support the exercise above:

Monitoring your own senses

The spiritual senses are experienced within and through the psychic faculties (your sensitivity) which every human being has. Therefore, within our mediumistical work, we can possess and experience all of the spiritual senses.

Are you working with all your spiritual senses?

SPIRITUAL SENSE	MEANING	YES/NO?
CLAIRVOYANCE	SEEING	
CLAIRAUDIENCE	HEARING	
CLAIRSENTIENCE	SENSING	
CLAIRGUSTANCE	TASTING	
CLAIRALIENCE	SMELLING	

As mediums, it is important from time to time to remind ourselves of all the senses within our sensitivity and to reconfirm that we have the potential to use all of them naturally at any given time within our mediumship.

Exercise 25

An exercise for advanced students

This exercise is suitable as a platform demonstration. The student should take time to attune to the spirit word and secure the blending with an individual from the spirit world and proceed with the demonstration. Once the medium has secured a recipient who, through the evidence offered up to the medium, understands who the communicator is, the medium is to proceed for a further minute, then invite a second communicator to step forward from the spirit world. As quickly as possible, the medium is to highlight how the first and second communicators are both connected to each other and to the recipient, and support this statement through factual evidence. This is to be followed by the message (reason for coming) and bringing the demonstration to an end. Discuss your findings and if necessary change roles and repeat the exercise.

Exercise 26

An exercise suitable for beginners

This exercise is suitable either as a group or as an exercise to be done on your own. Each student will need a pen and paper. There is no time limit on this exercise but it is important that the student be aware when the exercise naturally ends. Take time attuning yourself to the spirit world, keeping in your mind that the communicator who steps forward to blend with you will be one of your guides.

It is important that you don't interact or try to gather information from your guide but simply allow, as your guide steps forward from the spirit world, both yourself and your guide to blend and share the same space. For the next 5 minutes, through the power of your mind, I would like you to express to your guide what you would like for the future. This may be to do with your mediumship, your finances, your home life or whatever subject you like to talk about.

Once the 5 minutes have elapsed, I would like you to still your mind and allow your guide to step even closer to you. Pick up the pen and paper and begin to write, knowing that your guide will be inspiring you, with the words you are writing and expressing their thoughts on your future. It is important that you are disciplined at this stage of the exercise and do not influence the writing either with your thoughts or desires. Simply allow the guide's opinion to be expressed through the writing. After your guide has finished their answer and completed the letter, you can invite your guide to step away and read the letter as a recipient.

Exercise 27

An exercise suitable for intermediate students

This exercise is suitable for a one-to-one sitting environment and should last for 20 minutes. The student who is working first must firstly attune themselves to their recipient's auric field (i.e. work solely upon the psychic level).

As the student who is working perceives the information within the client's auric field, they are to verbalise what it is they are perceiving, which must continue for 10 minutes, during which time the student who is working is to be aware of their own energy and sensitivity (How does it feel? What is the movement and frequency of your energy whilst working psychically?)

Once the first 10 minutes has elapsed, the student is to take time to attune themselves to the spirit world and invite an individual to step forward from the spirit world who is related to the recipient, and continue the second 10 minutes with a mediumistical sitting, during which time the student is to be aware of their own energy and sensitivity (How does their energy and sensitivity differ from when working psychically, if at all?). After the second 10 minutes has drawn to a close, the student is to move to the message (reason for coming) and bring the sitting to an end. Discuss your findings (highlight the difference for you and your energy when working psychically and working mediumistically) and change roles.

Exercise 28

An exercise suitable for intermediate and advanced students

I have noticed over the years that I have taught mediumship, that a lot of students of mediumship put a lot of value on names within their mediumship (they want names as evidence to be a part of their mediumship. As a group, I would like you to discuss where in life we see names, because of course names are not only limited to people. We find names of our pets, names of roads, buildings – for example pubs – and it is important that you don't only limit yourself to names. For example don't forget titles, brands, breeds. Discuss this before starting the exercise.

This exercise is suitable in a one-to-one sitting setting. This exercise will be a 20-minute exercise and at any time during the sitting if a name, brand, make, breed, building, title naturally comes into the sitting as a piece of information, I would like you to take your attention back to the communicator and give a further statement: a story to support the said name, brand, title etc. and after approximately 15 minutes, naturally move to the message (reason for coming), bring the exercise to a close, discuss your findings and change roles.

Exercise 29

An exercise suitable for advanced students

This is suitable as a one-to-one sitting. The goal of this exercise is to enrich the spiritual senses we use within our mediumship. This will be a 20-minute sitting and after the student who is working has attuned themselves to the spirit world, made a link and begun to deliver information about the communicator they are aware of to their recipient for about ten minutes, they are to pick one of the senses (CLAIRVOYANCE, CLAIRSENTIENCE,

CLAIRAUDIENCE, CLAIRGUSTANCE or CLAIRALIENCE) and, to the best of their ability, use only that one sense for the following 5 minutes. After this 5 minutes has elapsed, naturally move into the reason for coming (message) and after you have completed this exercise move to a different recipient and repeat the exercise using a different sense to the one already used.

Of course, this exercise can be repeated five times using all the senses. On completion of this exercise, depending on your time restrictions and therefore how many of the senses you have covered, you can discuss your findings and change roles. Possibly the next time you are in each other's company you can repeat this exercise covering the senses you did not cover in the initial sitting.

CHAPTER 10

THE IMPORTANCE AND VALUE OF MEDITATION WITHIN YOUR MEDIUMSHIP

For centuries, meditation has been used as a discipline and practice to encourage the natural enfoldment and growth of spirituality within one's self. We only have to look to the eastern countries such as India, China and many more where we find meditation as a natural, entwined part of their culture and spiritual practices.

Within the belief systems, Buddhism and Hinduism, meditation is encouraged not for the benefit of mediumistical development but as a crucial part of spiritual enlightenment. If we look at the values and importance of meditation as part of the development of one's mediumship, it is a slightly different relationship and approach to meditation to those already mentioned.

Whilst for a student of mediumship, meditation will bring about and encourage clarity of spirituality within the mind and life of the student, it will equally give opportunity to both enrich the spiritual energies which the medium will naturally use during the process of mediumship.

So, let us look at the practice of meditation from a medium's point of view – a practical point of view, not a spiritual point of view. Each time you sit to meditate, you mentally move into an altered state of consciousness (the meditational state). Similarly, each time a medium practices mediumship, they move into an altered state of consciousness.

Each time a student meditates through the senses as part of the meditation, they are having experiences or at least very similar experiences to clairaudience, clairsentience and clairvoyance. In comparison, each time a medium practices mediumship they are having the experiences of perceiving individuals from the spirit world through the psychic senses clairaudience, clairsentience and clairvoyance.

From time to time during an individual's meditation, they will have the company of somebody from the spirit world, possibly a guide or family member who steps forward from the spirit world to be a part of the meditation. Comparatively, each time a medium demonstrates mediumship, they have the company of an individual from the spirit world.

Each time an individual sits for meditation they will naturally expand their spiritual energy (auric field) therefore enriching the clarity of that said spiritual energy and heightening their sensitivity. In comparison, each time a medium demonstrates mediumship they expand their spiritual energy (attunement) and work through and within their sensitivity.

So, we see there are many comparisons to be made within the disciplines of meditation and the practice of mediumship. From a practical point of view, each time you meditate it is like you are going to the gym to strengthen your mediumistical muscles. As a 19-year-old young man, starting out on my development of mediumship, my tutors, one of whom was a swami, insisted that I meditated once a day for approximately 30 minutes each time. Initially I struggled with the thought and the discipline of meditating daily, but very quickly I realised that I was lacking in the energy (fuel) required to be a competent medium, so reluctantly I disciplined myself to sit on a daily basis and within weeks I was aware of the improved clarity of energy during the practice of my mediumship which had a profound positive effect on my relationship with the spirit world, which in turn allowed the enfoldment of my mediumship to move forward in a more positive manner.

As a tutor of mediumship, I do always promote the practice of meditation as part of your spiritual and mediumistical unfoldment, however, over the years from time to time, students have approached me and expressed how they believe meditation is simply not for them.

Whilst we should accept that meditation on a regular basis is a discipline and therefore challenging for some depending on where you are at upon your path of development, I must encourage all students to at least look at meditation as part of their development within their mediumship. If you are one of those that find meditation a challenge, you are possibly practicing the wrong type of meditation to suit both your personality and the compatibility of your energy.

There are many different types of meditation that we can practice. Here are a few examples: contemplation, relaxation, sitting in the power and finally practical meditation.

Contemplation – this is a practice whereby the student would take a word, a phrase or a thought into the quietness of their own mind and, if you like, into a light state of meditation and contemplate that word, phrase or thought.

Relaxation – the development of mediumship can sometimes be mentally, emotionally and spiritually challenging and there are times when we need simply to relax to recharge our own batteries. Equally during the practice of mediumship, the consciousness should always be of a passive state so as not to influence the thoughts of the communicating spirit with one's own thoughts and the meditational practice known as relaxation can help you achieve the ideal state of mind that is compatible with mediumship.

Sitting in the power is a practice that does not involve

interacting with discarnate spirit and is very much mentally passive with none or very little interactions with the experiences during the duration of the practice but indeed involves the awareness of one's own spiritual energy (power) by focusing, dwelling and becoming aware of one's own spiritual power. This practice brings about the natural phenomena of enriching the clarity of that said power (spiritual energy) which can only help and improve the relationship one has with the spirit world. Secondly, think of yourself as an individual. Picture yourself in your mind with your auric field, during the practice of mediumship when an individual steps forward from the spirit world to blend with you. There is a blending of energies; a blending of the auric fields. With this in mind when sitting in the power over a sustained period of time, we acclimatise ourselves and familiarise ourselves with our own energy. This allows us to more readily recognise any changes within our auric field (power) that may come about due to the company of an individual from the spirit world.

Meditation comes in many different formats that quite often will have a goal and purpose. For example, maybe a tutor wishes for students to accept that within their mediumship lies the potential to work with all the senses. Therefore, the tutor will design a meditation that will involve the seeing, the hearing, the sensing, the tasting and the smelling. Meditation would normally be slightly more mentally interactive from the student's point of view with and during the meditation.

In these four different examples, the mental interaction and the spirit input differs from practice to practice, therefore the energy and the frequency of the energy would differ depending on the style and format of meditation.

If we look at this from a scientific point of view, the frequencies of energy within some practices may indeed be compatible with the student's energy and equally some may not, so it is important that you experiment with all the different types of meditation to find the style that is compatible both with your personality and your energy.

I can only encourage you, as a student of mediumship, to sit for meditation on a daily basis as it will bring depth and clarity to both your relationship with the spirit world and to the level of mediumship that you will naturally elevate yourself to.

Each meditation is very individual and unique and can sometimes have a profound effect upon you. Let me share with you a meditation that I experienced that had a profound effect upon me and an experience that will stay in my heart for many years.

For several years now I have been working in a mediumship school in the French speaking part of Switzerland, Neuchâtel, and on one particular visit several years ago, at a very stressful part in my life, I arrived early at the apartment I was staying at. The apartment sat at the edge of a beautiful lake, lake Neuchâtel, and feeling sorry for myself I thought I would take a walk around the lake.

It was a beautiful day and there were very few people at the lake this particular day, and along the side of the lake were placed what could only be described as very short tables. I guessed these were for the purpose of family picnics or for groups to sit upon. As I walked, I thought it would be pleasant to stop and meditate as I just wanted to feel the love and presence of the spirit world, so I sat upon one of these short tables, reached into my pocket for my iPhone which I had some meditational music on, plugged in my earphones, closed my eyes and started to meditate.

Quite quickly as part of the meditation I found myself on a mountain top. The clouds were beneath me and I could see in the distance the peaks of several other mountain tops and on one of the mountain peaks I could see several of my guides and I could feel them expressing their love towards me. I remember thinking in that moment, this is exactly what I wanted to experience from the spirit world, and little did I know what was to come. As I basked in the energy and love of my guides, suddenly I saw in my mind's eye, as part of the meditation, on a third mountain peak five swamis dressed in their full terracotta/orange robes, and very gently each of them put a hand into their robes, revealing very crude eastern musical instruments, and began to play music which in itself was of an eastern style yet was beautiful, and continued for approximately 30 minutes. Then I began to become aware that the music on my iPhone, which at this time was very much distant, was coming to an end.

This gently brought me out of the meditation and thus the meditation was finished. I opened my eyes, turned off my iPhone, put the phone and headphones back into my pocket, and stood up from the platform, stretching, and feeling very uplifted and full of the power of spirit, ready to face the days teaching I had in front of me.

As I turned to walk away to make my way back to the apartment, there, walking towards me, were five swamis dressed in their robes (remember I was no longer in the meditation) and I could see that they were purposely walking towards me. As they approached me, one of them, in broken English asked could they play some music to me and for a quick second in my mind I couldn't believe what was happening and I had to double check that I wasn't still in the meditation. No – I was fully conscious with five swamis standing right in front of me just like the meditation asking if they could play some music to me.

I replied, "Do you want to play music to me?" and their answer was "Yes, why not?" I said it would be a pleasure to listen to their music and I directed them to the platform and the spokesman said, "No, you sit on the platform, we will sit on the floor beneath you." Traditionally the student always sits beneath the swami. I sat on the platform and the five swamis made themselves comfortable on the floor in front of me, each of them revealing a crude eastern musical instrument from within their robes, just like in the meditation and they began to play their music for me, playing for about 30 minutes.

All the time during the playing of the music I could feel a healing energy washing over me and when the music had finished I asked them, "Why did you want to play music to me?" The spokesperson answered, "The spirit just directed us to you." He then went on to explain that in Neuchâtel that weekend was a musical festival and the five of them had flown over from India to share their music, and went on to present me with one of their CD's which I play from time to time to this day.

The power of meditation knows no boundaries. Anytime you have any challenges or problems within your mediumship or indeed your personal life, I would recommend you meditate on it, talk to the spirit world and seek their advice.

There is nothing you cannot resolve within the practice of meditation. If you are serious about the development of your mediumship, I recommend you meditate on a regular basis.

CHAPTER 11

STORIES AND EXPERIENCES ALONG THE WAY

When a medium decides to take his or her mediumship public and becomes a working medium and possibly beyond that a professional medium, there will be challenges and unusual experiences that one will have over and beyond the mediumship. So, let me share some of my stories and experiences I have had along the way.

The following story is a memory that will stay with me forever because of how real and factual it was for me. As a young man, I desperately failed with my education and my relationship with my secondary school and at the age of 15, my teachers lost their patience with me and I was excluded from school. Quite quickly I secured some work for a roofing firm as a labourer for two men: Eddie and Chris (who was known as Bushy). They were two straight talking, hard working men.

One of the first jobs I worked on with them was on a house on Crab Tree Lane, Fulham, London. This house had stood empty for several years and the new owner had employed Eddie and Bushy to put on a new roof, install a new kitchen and bathroom, and to clean out a basement that was full of rubbish.

On one particular day at lunch time, I took myself with my sandwiches my mother had made me for dinner up to the first-floor landing whilst Eddie and Bushy went off to the pub for lunch, and as I was sitting on the bare floorboards happily eating my sandwiches, I heard objectively, footsteps coming up the staircase, which were the footsteps of a young man who looked about 17 years of age.

He stopped on the stairs and started to talk to me, myself one side of the stair spindles whilst the young man was on the other side. As we engaged in conversation he enquired what was happening with the house. I explained that some building work was taking place within the house and how somebody had just recently purchased it.

The tone of his voice suddenly changed as if he was emotionally pleading with me, asking "please make sure you do a very good job of this house" and "please take care of this house" as if there was some emotional connection between the young man and the property. He then went on to ask if he could help with the work, and I explained to him that I was only a labourer on this firm and it wasn't for me to decide who worked there and who didn't work there.

We were no more than three feet apart and had spent approximately 5 minutes talking to each other, when he literally disappeared in front of my eyes. I did no more than to run down the stairs and out of the house and across the road petrified with the reality that I had just spent 5 minutes talking to a spirit, and in my own mind refusing to go back into the house.

After about 30 minutes, Eddie and Bushy returned from the pub and asked me what was I doing across the road and not continuing with my work. I simply shouted through my fear, "There's a ghost in that house!" Eddie clipped me round the back of the head and said, "Don't be so stupid, go and get on with your work," which hesitantly I did, the house now absent of the young man.

The very next day Eddie and Bushy had told me my work for the day was to clean out the cellar within the house, which over the years had been filled with rubbish. There was a skip that had been put outside the house and my job was to fill the skip and clean the cellar out. The cellar, from floor to ceiling was about five feet high, there was no lighting and it was full of dirt and dust. Hoarded inside, there was lots of broken furniture that had obviously been stored there over the years.

After about two hours of working in the cellar, I came across two large pictures and as I dragged the pictures out of the cellar and into the sunlight I realised they were both old black and white photographs. Because of how similar they both were it was obvious they had been taken within seconds of each other. The photographs were of a World War 1 regiment – approximately 16 young soldiers who had posed for the photograph.

As I examined the pictures, I was drawn to one of the young men in the photographs as I thought it was the young man who had stood on the staircase yesterday talking to me. That thought very quickly left my mind and my thoughts turned to the fact that these photographs could be worth some money, but where would I sell them? Maybe the library which was across town would be interested in having them?

That lunch time, with both photographs under my arms I marched across Fulham to the library which was a good 20-minute walk and on entering the library I met a lady who worked there and I asked would she be interested in purchasing these two photographs. She very quickly and firmly replied "no!" However, she said if I was interested she would research the photographs through the use of the library archives and if I would return the next day at the same time she could tell me more about the pictures.

I didn't particularly want to carry the two pictures all the way back across town so I reluctantly agreed. The next day I met up with the lady as agreed and she explained that at the beginning of WW1 especially in the inner-city areas of England, regiments were formed from streets and this regiment was known as the Crab Tree Regiment and I quickly explained to the lady that it was in Crab Tree Lane where I found the photographs. She went on to explain that sadly none of the young men in the photograph returned home and they all died in battle.

At that moment, the reality of the last few days hit me. The young man who had spoken to me on the staircase was obviously someone who had lived in that house, gone off to war and sadly never came home again, and the spirit of that young man was simply enquiring and concerned for the wellbeing of his home.

* * *

Like most mediums, as a young man I was desperate to demonstrate my mediumship publicly and was prepared to accept and do any services that were offered to me and, like most mediums who are new, I had grand ideas about how far I was going to take my mediumship.

For the first year or so, my public work was restricted to the Cambridgeshire area, all the time desperate to branch out to show the whole world how good I was. Then out of the blue I had a phone call from a lady who ran a church in Luton offering me a demonstration evening at her church. Here was an opportunity to show the world outside Cambridge how good I was, and of course I accepted the invite immediately.

The big day came in mid-October. I drove down to Luton with the address in hand thinking all the time that I'd successfully become a travelling medium and I was about to demonstrate, I'm sure, in one of the big spiritualist churches in Luton. However, on arrival I found myself parked outside a very large tin hut, the sign above the door suggested it was a scout's hut and obviously rented once a week by a local spiritualist group.

The tin hut had obviously stood in that location for some years. It was old, discoloured and slightly lopsided, possibly subsiding on one side. I was met by a small and lovely group of ladies who were the organisers of this event. There was a gathering of about

35-40 people who were attending the evening and the evening got underway.

I have to point out that all the time on this cold October evening the wind was battering the building quite severely, and at the entrance to this building were two large doors which did not sit within the frames correctly. Obviously over the years they had become worn and distorted, and as the wind blew the doors kept opening and slamming.

This was a lovely group of people and I was sure I could deal with these small disturbances. After one or two songs, the demonstration of mediumship began. All the time the double doors were repeatedly banging. Nonetheless here was my opportunity to show the world what a wonderful medium I was. The first two messages went fine and I thought I was on a roll, but as I started my third message, with the doors continually banging, suddenly I heard a disturbance in the aisle of the building. There in front of me was quite a large man who was obviously very drunk and very distressed. Later on I would discover that this man had split up with his wife that morning, left his house and gone and got drunk, and because he was a spiritualist, that evening he headed straight for the church.

As he stood in the middle of the aisle he began to raise his voice, moaning about an individual that he loved yet, in his opinion, she did not care about him. At this point I said to him, "If you sit down sir, I will talk to you after the demonstration." Some of the elderly ladies in the church began to panic and tried to cater to him. All the time in my mind I was thinking this man is disturbing my golden opportunity.

Suddenly the man fell to the floor, lying motionless yet continuing to mumble and complain about his wife. Two of the ladies stood up from their chairs and quickly went to his aid. Thinking my world was falling apart I shouted at the ladies, "Leave him, he can't fall any further than he is now," and they returned to their seats. The evening unfolded like a double act, me and the drunk.

For example the next message I gave was from a father who had passed years before. The recipient of the message was the daughter and as I was explaining to the daughter how much the father, whilst alive, had supported and loved her, the drunk, still from his lying position in the aisle shouted, "And you always hated me." I quickly explained to the daughter, "That's not what your father is saying, that's what the drunk is saying."

The next message was from a grandmother who was talking about the house that she had left and the decision by the family to sell the house so as to be able to divide the finances of the house between the members of the family. Of course in mid demonstration the drunk shouted with a very loud voice, "And you spent all that money I gave you." By this time I had given up on trying to be the superstar and began to see the funny side of this situation. With each following message I gave that evening I was supported one way or another by loud statements from the resident drunk which of course the whole congregation found very amusing.

At the end of the evening we lifted the man into a chair, gave him several cups of coffee, listened to his story and then sent him on his way. By this time, it was beginning to get quite late in the evening and I still had a long drive home, with home being a small remote village in Cambridgeshire. I said my goodbyes and started the journey home, feeling disheartened about the whole evening, thinking "maybe the spirit world just don't love me" and "maybe I'm not a superstar after all".

As I drove into the night, the wind continued to blow and the rain poured down through the whole of my journey. The journey ahead was going to take several hours and some way into the journey I began to feel very tired and found myself closing my eyes and drifting off whilst still driving the car. Suddenly, I physically felt a thump to my chest, at the same time hearing the words in an assertive voice, "You may not care about yourself but what about Elaine?" (Elaine being the name of my first wife). Amazed and astonished, this woke me up and made me fully alert once again which allowed me to continue my journey thinking as I drove along, "Wow, maybe the spirit world do love me after all".

About an hour after this experience and about 10 miles from home at about 1am, I found myself driving through a small village, the rain still pouring down, and there in the darkness at the side of the road was a young man thumbing a lift. Feeling sorry for him out in the cold and rain I pulled over, wound the window down and said, "What direction are you going?" and the young man, who was as physically solid as you or I leaned in the window and replied "I'm going your way Tim." Immediately, I wondered how he knew my name. I'd never met this man before, so how did he know my name? It quickly left my mind as I invited him into the car.

There I was, in the middle of the night driving with a complete stranger who started to talk to me with knowledge of me, always referring to me by my first name of which I hadn't offered him. His first statement to me was, "How are Elaine and the girls?" which was followed by directing me through the streets, each direction being the correct one to my journey, of which of course he had no knowledge of, all the time talking to me of people and events that were personal to me that a stranger would have no knowledge of.

We started to approach a T-junction and the young man pointed out that I was turning right at the T-junction and he was going left. He said thank you for the lift but that he would get out at that junction. As I stopped at the junction he turned to me, looked into my eyes and said, "Tim, remember, always look after yourself, and always look after your family." He opened the door, stepped out of the car and disappeared: literally disappeared into thin air. We were in a rural setting, no houses, no building for him to walk behind and he just literally disappeared. Maybe the drunk in the church and maybe the young man who shared my journey were sent by the spirit world to accompany me on my journey of both mediumship, which on that night was not what I expected it to be, and on my drive home, which also was not what I expected it to be. Maybe just like that day, the spirit world will always challenge us with good intentions but will also be by our side to keep us safe to the best of their ability.

* * *

As a tutor of mediumship, I have been asked many times over the years how soon can somebody communicate from the spirit world after they pass away and hopefully the following story will give the answer to that question.

Sometime in the late 1990s, I was doing a tour of Kent which included several one-day workshops, a demonstration of mediums, a divine service and several one-to-one private sittings. Part of my timetable was to take the Sunday divine service for Dover spiritualist church which was to be followed on the Monday by six private sittings, and the second sitting was with a lady I had never met before. For the sake of this story and her privacy we shall call her Sue, however, months later, I would learn that she was the cousin of a student of mine and I would also learn the incredible story that lay behind what seemed to be a regular clairvoyant sitting.

After Sue had arrived for the sitting and I had introduced myself and explained what was about to take place within the structure of the sitting, I very quickly became aware of a lady from the spirit world who explained to me that she had died suddenly. She gave me her name, a loose description of herself, how she loved craftwork, for example, knitting, sewing and crocheting and that she was mother to Sue. After offering this information up to Sue she replied by saying, "I can accept all that information with my mother Tim. However my mother is fine, I only left her 10 minutes ago and she is fine." My response was, "Well maybe it's not your mother, let me just get some more information from this lady to see if the facts fit for somebody else." After giving several more pieces of information to Sue, again she responded, "All that information fits my mother, but I know she's fine I've just left her."

After several minutes of persevering with further information from this lady from the spirit world and Sue not being able to place the information with anybody other than her mother who, as far as she was concerned, was absolutely fine and home, not wanting to spoil Sue's sitting, I invited the lady in the spirit world to step back to see if there was anybody else who wished to communicate, not something I would normally do. However, immediately I became aware of a gentleman who through information given to me, allowed Sue to accept him as her uncle.

One of the things Sue's uncle wished to talk about was Sue's mother, highlighting that Sue's mother was OK now. We continued with the duration of the sitting, brought it to an end and after a small chat, Sue thanked me and left. Several months later whilst teaching some students, during the dinner break a female student approached me and introduced herself as Sue's cousin and proceeded to share some further information which followed the sitting with Sue and the story.

After the sitting, Sue returned home, and upon entering the home she discovered her mother sadly dead in the very chair where she had left her minutes before the sitting. Because of Sue and her cousin's knowledge of the spirit world they were comfortable for me to know and share the story. Here was a mother who could only have been in the spirit world 10 minutes and was simply trying to tell her daughter that she was OK.

How long does it take for somebody to communicate after the point of physical death? I will leave that for you to decide.

* * *

As a tutor of mediumship I have had the pleasure of working for some beautiful organisations and people, one of which is Fréquences Swiss School of Mediumship. I have worked here for several years and continue to do so. This consists of several weekend seminars throughout the year, and on each visit, the accommodation is provided by a very kind and lovely lady called Dorothy.

On one trip to Dorothy's, upon entering the apartment I became aware of the spirit of a small very elderly lady and I was aware that this lady had only recently passed and, after enquiring with Dorothy about this lady, it was revealed to me that one of Dorothy's neighbours fitting that description had only recently passed. As I began to settle in and unpack my suitcase Dorothy asked me when it was I was returning back to England, and I replied, "Not until Monday evening."

The weekend unfolded as normal and on the Saturday evening whilst sitting having a coffee with Dorothy, she explained to me that the lady I had seen in the hallway was being buried on Monday and her family would be holding the wake in the hotel opposite Dorothy's apartment. She went on to explain to me how none of the elderly lady's family spoke English, however they loved the English language and were curious about my work with the spirit world and asked if I would like to attend the wake.

Immediately the alarm bells began to ring in my head as I thought I was going to be the entertainment at a wake, so "no" I said to Dorothy, "I have to journey home early Monday morning." Dorothy replied, "Oh I thought you were going Monday evening Tim." Petrified that I was going to have to do some sort of mediumship during a wake, I lied to Dorothy and said, "No, I have to go early in the morning." She volunteered to drive me to the train station on the Monday morning and of course I had to accept her offer.

Monday came and true to her word, Dorothy took me to the train station whereby I took a train to Geneva airport, arriving at the airport eight hours early for my flight and there was no way I was going to sit in an airport for eight hours, so I approached the airline customer service to enquire if I could exchange my ticket for an earlier flight and the representative explained that they wouldn't do that for me and there were no flights earlier that day back to Manchester, where my car was parked in the airport car park. However, the airline did inform me that in two hours' time there would be a flight to Gatwick and that would be my only choice other than going on my original flight.

So, at the cost of £200 I purchased a flight to Gatwick, but there was a problem – I needed to get from Gatwick to Manchester airport to collect my car. "Not a problem," the customer services rep said, "we can sell you a train ticket from Gatwick into London, and then from on from London to Manchester airport." So, at the cost of a further £50 I bought a train ticket.

Two hours later I was on my way. We arrived at Gatwick on time, then jumped on the train to central London where I would change trains to Manchester airport. All was going well – I found the train I needed and as I was about to enter the platform where the train to Manchester airport was standing, a railway guard asked to see my ticket and as he looked at my ticket he said, "Oh no, this won't do, this ticket is only for off peak times." The train was ready to go and I needed to act there and then or miss my train, so I asked the guard, "Well what can I do about this?" he pointed me in the direction of the ticket office around the corner where they could advise me, which they did... A further £50...

This journey was starting to become quite expensive. Nonetheless I caught the train and made my way to Manchester airport and phoned the meet & greet firm that housed my car whilst I was in Switzerland, and because I was in Manchester airport at a different time than I would have been if taking the original flight the meet & greet firm explained it was going to take some time for them to get my car to me. It took approximately 30 minutes. I had just one hour's car drive ahead of me and then I would be home. On arriving at home, my wife who had no knowledge of the story that had been unfolding asked me "Was the flight delayed? Because you're running an hour late." I had arrived home an hour later than if I'd have waited and caught my original flight. I was £300 worse off, which was the cost of the original flight and I took a journey around England just so I didn't have to entertain at a wake. A few years later I picked up the courage to tell Dorothy the true story – again I'm sorry Dorothy.

* * *

During the years that I have worked as a medium I have had the pleasure of working in and visiting many different countries and in 2010 I had the pleasure of running a seminar in the beautiful country of Iceland. This visit to Iceland involved me being there for a good week. Whilst I was there my organiser and host was a lovely elderly lady with the nickname of Fifi, whom I loved dearly.

On arrival, Fifi explained to me that the country was under threat by a very large volcano, Eyjafjallajökull, which did indeed erupt whilst I was there, but the students were there so the work had to go ahead. After completing the seminar, I had a day off before flying home and Fifi asked me, "Is there anything in particular you would like to do on your day off Tim?" I replied, "I would love to go and see the volcano, because how often does an Englishman get the opportunity to get up close to a live volcano?" "Not a problem," she said, "a student of mine lives at the foot of mountain where the volcano is."

She went on to explain to me that she would take me at night time so the effect of the volcano would be greater. So the next evening we set off into the darkness. Several hours drive across Iceland, and as we drove in the dark, way off in the distance I could see the volcano erupting like a fantastic firework display. After several hours, we arrived at a dairy farm, which was indeed at the foot of the mountain that housed the live volcano. The dairy farm was owned by a husband and wife, of which the wife was a student of Fifi's.

We knocked on the door of the farm and were greeted by the husband who explained to us that his wife was out working on the farm and would be back shortly, but he invited us in and made us a coffee and he introduced us to a young man (for the sake of the story we will name him Johnny). Johnny was a very angry American teenager who was a student exchange and was staying at the farm for several weeks. Unfortunately, every other word that Johnny spoke was a swear word, but hey, I was there to see the volcano.

After approximately 15 minutes the wife entered the room, a tall slender lady whose dress code suggested she was a bit of a hippy. She came straight over and greeted us, and immediately asked me, "Did you think that mother was angry?" My reply was, "Sorry, I don't know your mother," and she said, "No Tim, you don't understand, follow me and I will explain." The hippy woman, Fifi, the angry American and myself went out into her farmyard in the darkness of the night, and there on the floor were about a dozen boulders, each one roughly the size of a bowling ball.

The hippy woman pointed to them and said, "Look Tim, I've been up the mountain and brought back some of the babies. Do you think Mother is angry?" All the time of course in the background there is a volcano on the top of a mountain spewing lava everywhere. "Not at all," I explained, "This is a natural phenomenon, the volcano is neither sad nor happy." The hippy lady then proceeded by saying, "Then could we say a prayer to the volcano, explaining to the volcano that we are looking after her children?" Immediately a thought crossed my mind – I haven't been paid yet for the seminar. "Yes of course we can say a prayer," I said, so the hippy, Fifi, the angry American and myself held hands around the boulders whilst looking at the erupting volcano and I said out loud the following prayer: "Dear mother, we have your children, and I give you my word, we will look after them, here in their new home, with their new family at the foot of your mountain. Amen."

This prayer did not seem to have any effect on the volcano at all, as it just continued spewing out lava into the night sky. However, everybody who was present was satisfied with the prayer and now was the time to journey up the mountain. The hippy lady explained she had just the vehicle for the job, and disappeared into a neighbouring barn. Suddenly the largest 4x4 vehicle I think I have ever seen appeared being driven by the hippy woman. Fifi climbed in the front as Johnny and myself climbed in the back, and off we went.

Probably within 10 minutes we found ourselves in a traffic jam and it seemed that everybody in Iceland had the same idea – they all wanted to climb the mountain to see the volcano. There were young men on mopeds, coaches full of people, cars ill prepared for mountain climbing, and even a helicopter in the sky. After a few moments of being stationary the hippy woman, growing impatient said, "I've got an idea," and turned sharp right and drove straight across a field heading higher and higher up the mountain. At one point we even crossed a river.

Whilst Iceland is a beautiful country those of you who know Iceland well will know that when you get off the main roads it becomes very rugged and bumpy so our journey up the mountainside from start to finish was a bumpy one. All the time Johnny by the side of me, who obviously wasn't enjoying the journey, was openly cursing, whilst the two ladies in the front, being of a spiritual nature, were engrossed with the energy of the volcano and all I could hear from them was, "Wow, can you feel the energy Tim?" Because of the continuous bumping I was not concerning myself with the energy but more concerned with staying seated in my chair.

After about 30 minutes of continuous cursing by the side of me and hearing the same question from in front of me all I needed was to use the toilet, so I found myself holding my crotch whilst bouncing up and down up a mountain. A further 30 minutes up the mountainside and we found ourselves on an ice plateau about half a mile from a lava river. We brought the car to a stop, as immediately I said to the ladies in front, "I need to go round the back of the car so I can go to the toilet." They were so engrossed with the volcano I don't think they heard my statement because their reply was simply, "Wow, can you feel that energy?" All this time Johnny was complaining.

I climbed out of the car to relieve myself, to be faced by the most intense heat I have ever experienced, whilst at the same time this heat was supported by the most amazing energy I have every witnessed, and as I stood at the back of the car with my manly bits in hand, staring at the lava river in the distance, suddenly I became aware of somebody standing by the side of me and a voice that said, "Wow, isn't that powerful?" It was Fifi and for a split moment I wondered whether she was talking about me or the lava river…

I very quickly put my bits away and I don't know if Fifi ever saw what she shouldn't have seen but it was never ever mentioned again. What I do know is that as mediums we preach about the power and the beauty of the spirit world but we must never forget how powerful and beautiful our own world is.

✳ ✳ ✳

The stories I have shared with you are but a few experiences I have had over the years. I think it's important to remember that spiritualism and mediumship are an expression of life and have nothing to do with death and hopefully these few stories have expressed that.

CHAPTER 12

CLOSING THOUGHTS

I only hope that as you have journeyed through both the subjects and exercises laid out in this book that you feel in some way it has helped to enrich both your knowledge of mediumship and your mediumistical ability. At the end of the day, no book, teacher or organisation can be responsible for your development, and how far you take your mediumistical ability is solely your responsibility. At each opportunity, push back any barriers that you may find within your mediumship and adopt the approach that there are no limitations to what you can achieve and I do hope that this book has helped you to do that very thing.

All that is in this book is simply my opinion and if you find anything within this book that insults your intelligence please discard it. However, if you find anything within this book that inspires you and you feel will enrich your mediumship please don't simply look at it or practise it once – indeed practise it several times so it becomes a natural part of your mediumship. I would love to hear from you as to how you feel this book has helped you, or indeed any thoughts or opinions you have on this book.

Remember – Together,
Let's Raise the Standards!

**Books and CDs I would like to recommend
for your reading and education are:**

How to be a Medium – W.H. Evans

The unseen self – Brian Snellgrove

The University of Spiritualism – Harry Boddington

Simply Mediumship – A beginner's guide
- Minister Martin Colclough

Simply Trance Mediumship – A beginner's
guide - Minister Martin Colclough

And, of course, my first book:
Mediumship – Raising the Standards by Tim Abbott

Also, check out the meditational CDs by Libby
Clark OSNU and of Shelia French DSNU

**But not forgetting my CD
Enhancing the senses through the power of meditation**

Please visit my website
www.timabbott.net
for any further details you may require